国家林业和草原局普通高等教育"十四五"规划教材
国家级精品在线课程"外经贸英语函电"配套教材

外经贸英语函电实训教程

张云清 主 编

中国林业出版社
China Forestry Publishing House

内 容 简 介

本教材以国际贸易业务流程知识为理论背景,通过做中学的方式,对外经贸英语函电的一般格式、常用词汇、习惯表达法进行规律性的总结,是一门理论与实践紧密结合、具有涉外活动特点的综合应用性教材。本教材首先介绍中国的外贸发展历史以及贸易交易会的相关知识;然后以任务为驱动,从建交、价格谈判、订单与合同、付款方式、包装、运输、保险、索赔与理赔等环节,引导学生进行线上和线下的进出口贸易函电以及单证实训。本教材将中国古代经商故事与中国现代特色农产品的出口案例相结合,并在实际教学课程中配以虚拟仿真技术,进行实景农产品商务谈判实践,以此实现立体化教学。此外,基于校企合作,本教材的函电例文大多采用企业最新的真实外贸文本,以此体现教材的实用性与先进性。

图书在版编目(CIP)数据

外经贸英语函电实训教程/张云清主编. —北京:中国林业出版社,2023.5(2024.2重印)
国家林业和草原局普通高等教育"十四五"重点规划教材
国家级精品在线课程"外经贸英语函电"配套教材
ISBN 978-7-5219-2040-6

Ⅰ. ①外… Ⅱ. ①张… Ⅲ. ①对外贸易-英语-电报信函-写作-高等学校-教材 Ⅳ. ①F75

中国版本图书馆 CIP 数据核字(2022)第 254196 号

策划编辑:曹鑫茹
责任编辑:曹鑫茹 王奕丹
责任校对:苏 梅
封面设计:睿思视界视觉设计

出版发行:中国林业出版社
　　　　(100009,北京市西城区刘海胡同7号,电话 83223120)
电子邮箱:cfphzbs@163.com
网　　址:www.forestry.gov.cn/lycb.html
印　　刷:北京中科印刷有限公司
版　　次:2023年5月第1版
印　　次:2024年2月第2次印刷
开　　本:787mm×1092mm　1/16
印　　张:10
字　　数:265千字
定　　价:42.00元

《外经贸英语函电实训教程》编写人员

主　编　张云清

编　者　（按姓氏拼音排序）
　　　　陈尾云（福建农林大学金山学院）
　　　　黄丽莉（福建农林大学）
　　　　李秀芬（福建仙芝楼医药科技有限公司）
　　　　陶　媛（福州外语外贸学院）
　　　　姚　静（福建农林大学）
　　　　于　琼（福州大学）
　　　　游金干（福建农林大学金山学院）
　　　　张云清（福建农林大学）

前言
Preface

自 2010 年以来，教育部出台了一系列重要政策文件，如《教育信息化十年发展规划（2011—2020 年）》（2012）、《教育信息化"十三五"规划》（2016）、《教育部高等教育司 2022 年工作要点》（2022）等，均从不同层面提出高等教育信息化、数字化改革的重要性和迫切性。2022 年，党的二十大报告提出了"以中国式现代化全面推进中华民族伟大复兴"的使命，并首次把教育、科技、人才进行"三位一体"统筹部署，极具战略意义和深远影响。促进外语教育教材建设的高质量发展，我们要以"立德树人"为根本任务，坚持创新发展理念，要大胆探索智能技术与外语教育深度融合，充分挖掘教育教学优质资源，服务地方经济社会发展多元需求，服务学生个性化发展多元需求。

《外经贸英语函电实训教程》是基于《外经贸英语函电》在线开放课程而开发的实践拓展性配套纸质教材。作为福建省首批精品在线开放课程，自 2015 年建设以来，《外经贸英语函电》先后在超星泛雅平台以及爱课程中国大学 MOOC 网上架开课。选课高校从 2016—2017 学年的 8 所，增至 2017—2018 年的 132 所，2018 年年底被评为国家级精品在线开放课程，2020 年获得国家级一流课程认定，选课人数目前已经超过 5 万人，选课院校超过 200 所。

本教材以"内生育人"为驱动，基于"教师主导、学生主体、内容为纲"的教育理念，跨文化沟通技能与商务写作技能相结合，将国际贸易与英语相结合，同时注重理想信念、文化素养、道德品质以及职业素养的教育。教材首先确立拓展国际贸易知识、提升商务写作能力、加强跨学科综合素养的教学目标，并进一步融入思政元素，如中国特色社会主义道路、中国梦、生态伦理观、职业道德观、和谐人际观等，从而在深度和广度上引导学生正确对待中西文化差异，树立良好的职业道德，增强文化自信，提升跨文化商务交际能力。

教育部副部长吴岩曾指出"教材质量"属于"新文科"人才培养的"主要剧本"。本教材通过"三高、四结合、三融合"来体现特色与创新。

1. 三高

第一，课程起点高。本教材是基于国家级精品在线开放课程《外经贸英语函电》编写的纸质配套教材。要求学生能够立足中国、立足新阶段，了解当代中国贸易的特点。第二，培养理念高。本教材结合中国案例，以任务为驱动，体现"学生中心、产出导向、多元评价"的先进培养理念。第三，内容要求高。本教材通过校企合作，基于企业提供的真实案例，编写具有时代特征的最新函电文本，体现与时俱进的规范性文本内容。并要求结合一流慕课资源、电子习题库、虚拟仿真实验平台，体现数字人文理念，以此推进一流课程建设。

2. 四结合

第一，结合"双万计划"。本教材将服务于国家级一流课程建设，提升《外经贸英语函电》慕课学习的深度和广度。第二，结合"新文科"建设。本教材内容涉及农产品知识、国际贸易知识、商务英语语言表达、商务沟通技巧、跨文化交际能力，体现了"跨界融合"的新文科特点，有助于推进新文科下的外语课程改革创新。第三，结合课程思政。每个单元设有明确的情感目标，来培养学生正确的职业道德观、人际和谐观以及社会责任感。第四，结合通识教育，通过做中学，培养学生健全的人格，提升创新实践能力、沟通表达能力。最终为培养"懂中国、懂世界、懂自我、懂社会"的卓越人才贡献力量。

3. 三融合

本教材通过校内外融合（课程学习与企业实践）、学科专业融合（国际贸易和英语）、线上线下融合（慕课基础学习、虚拟仿真实景实践、课堂深入研讨反思），培养具有"语言知识、人文素养、学科特色、跨文化能力"的高层次、国际化复合型人才。

本教材遵循"学生中心、产出导向"的教学方法设计，通过设定国际贸易产出任务以及知识、能力和情感的三维学习目标，采用"做中学"方式，帮助学生了解自身不足、激发学习动力、培养合作能力。本教材通过任务驱动、学习目标、知识要点、语言表达、案例分析以及技能实训 6 个模块，从内容组织、语篇结构、语言技巧、商务知识等方面为学生提供有效的补充，并通过科学地练习设计引导学生把理论与实践相结合，最终学会学以致用。

本教材既可以作为英语专业商务方向或商务英语专业的核心教材，也可以作为国际贸易专业的配套教材，同时满足非英语专业学生的通识教育需求。与国家级线上一流课程《外经贸英语函电》配套使用，开展线上线下混合式教学，效果将更加突出。

本教材第一章由姚静和陶媛编写；第二章到第九章，黄丽莉和游金干负责编写案例分析，陈尾云负责编写技能实训中的拓展阅读，张云清负责编写学习目标、知识要点、语言表达，张云清和于琼负责编写技能实训；本教材的参考文献、习题答案以及内容整合均由张云清完成。此外，本教材在编写过程中得到福建仙芝楼医药科技有限公司李秀芬总经理的大力支持，为本教材提供了各类函电来往案例和单据。同时感谢向琴博士、游金干老师、吴丹丹和黄艺莹同学为本教材进行语法、语言以及格式修订。

由于编者水平有限，书中错漏或者不当之处在所难免，敬请各位读者不吝指正，以便未来进一步修改和完善。

编　者
2022 年 10 月

目 录
Contents

Preface

Chapter 1 Introduction ··· 1

Chapter 2 Establishing Business Relations ································· 23

Chapter 3 Price Negotiation (Enquiry, Offer & Counter-offer) ····· 37

Chapter 4 Order and Contract ·· 52

Chapter 5 Payment and Documentation ································· 67

Chapter 6 Packing ··· 84

Chapter 7 Shipment ·· 99

Chapter 8 Insurance ·· 114

Chapter 9 Claim and Settlement ·· 128

Bibliography ·· 141

Appendix One ··· 143

Appendix Two ··· 146

扫码获取
参考答案

Chapter 1 Introduction

Task Driven

South Africa Sprout International Corporation plans to participate in the China International Agricultural Trade Fair (CATF). The sales representative, Mr. Will Smith, would like to know more about CATF, including its establishment date, scale and impact. Students are required to work in groups to collect information about CATF via Internet.

Learning Objectives

• **Knowledge objectives:** Understand the history and current development of China's foreign trade; Grasp the function of trade fair, the selection of trade fair, and the preparation and business etiquette needed for attending trade fair.

• **Skill objectives:** Collect, analyze and summarize business information.

• **Affective objectives:** Communicate with business partners in a courteous manner.

Core Concept

1.1 A Brief History of China's Foreign Trade

China's foreign trade began in the pre-Qin period, flourished in the Song and Yuan Dynasties, but waned in the late Qing Dynasty. Over the past 70 years since the founding of the People's Republic of China, especially since the reform and opening-up, the country's foreign trade has developed rapidly. In recent years, China's foreign trade volume ranks the top in the world.

Strictly speaking, ancient China's foreign trade began in the Western Han Dynasty. At that time, there were two ways to connect with the outside world. One was an overland route to the Western Regions, known as the "Silk Road"; the other was a mantime route from the South China Sea to coastal areas, known as the "Maritime Silk Road". The two "Silk Roads" greatly promoted the trade contacts between the Western Han Dynasty and the Central Asian countries in the Western Regions. According to *The Book of the Han Dynasty*, when Zhang Qian, an envoy of the Western Han Dynasty, visited the Western Regions, he brought back grapes, pomegranates, cucumbers, walnuts, coriander, flax and carrots and other products from the Western Regions, as well as sugarcane, spices and herbs from East and Southeast Asia, which greatly enriched the plant varieties of China.

During the Wei, Jin, Northern and Southern Dynasties, Sino-foreign economic exchanges developed further both in depth and in breadth. Silk was the most exported commodity. In addition, porcelain, lacquer, bronze, jade, peach, apricot and other fruits, cinnamon, rhubarb, coptis and other medicinal materials and tea were also exported.

In Tang Dynasty, the feudal politics and economy developed rapidly and foreign trade was flourishing, and Chang'an became the center of economic and cultural exchanges among Asian countries. The imperial court had special agencies responsible for foreign trade administration. The Tang Dynasty attached importance to both sea and land transportation. At that time, there were land and water routes to Korea and Japan in the east, the "Silk Road" in the west led to present-day India, Iran, Arabia and many European countries, and the "Maritime Silk Road" led to the Persian Gulf. In addition, with the rapid economic development in south China and the advanced technology of navigation and shipbuilding, foreign trade was increasingly dependent on maritime traffic.

The Song and Yuan Dynasties witnessed the development of foreign trade in feudal China. The governments of both dynasties encouraged foreign trade to increase fiscal revenue. As foreign trade was frequent, the imperial court set up the Market and Ship Department to manage foreign trade. There were two main ways of foreign trade: One is official trade in the name of "tributary trade", and the other is civilian trade. Important ports at that time included Guangzhou, Quanzhou, and etc. In addition, Korea, Japan and Vietnam were main foreign trade partners to China.

Ming Dynasty was the turning point of China's foreign trade from prosperity to decline. A strict ban on maritime trade policy was implemented in the early Ming Dynasty to forbid individuals to do business overseas and foreign businessmen to trade in China. Meanwhile, "tributary trade" was regarded as the only legal form of foreign trade. Zheng He's seven voyages to the Western world during the Ming Dynasty greatly strengthened China's economic ties with Asian and African countries. However, the long-term maritime prohibition policy seriously destroyed the development of social economy and the germination of capitalism.

The Qing Dynasty continued the maritime prohibition policy of the Ming Dynasty to a certain extent in its early years, and imposed strict restrictions on overseas trade. However, under the closed-door policy, China's foreign trade lost its initiative, the economic vitality was severely restricted, and the economic development became increasingly sluggish. After the Opium War, the Chinese market was increasingly opened to foreign powers, and foreign goods and capital poured into China. With the gradual disintegration of natural economy, China gradually became a semi-colonial and semi-feudal society.

Since the founding of the People's Republic of China, foreign economic and trade relations have undergone an important historic turning point. China has ended the unequal and exploited international trade status in the semi-colonial and semi-feudal society, and emerged the international economic and trade with an equal and independent identity, and began to occupy a pivotal position in the world economy. After 60 years of development since the founding of the People's Republic of China, the country's foreign trade has formed five basic characteristics by 2010. In terms of trade structure, trade in goods is the main content of foreign trade, while trade in services is weak. With regard to trade in goods, the export-oriented strategy has taken the lead, and the export scale has obviously and continuously exceeded the import scale. In terms of capital flows, China attracts foreign investment on a large scale and now becomes a net capital inflow country. As for opening to the outside world, the country's key open areas are still mainly in the eastern coastal areas, and inland cities have also begun to open gradually. When it comes to world economic status, China focuses on following the rules of the world economy and remains a follower of the world economy.

Since 2010, with China's growing economic power and the proposal and continuous progress of the "Belt and Road Initiative", China's foreign trade and even economic development have entered a new stage of qualitative and profound transformation and demonstrate five new characteristics. (1) The trade structure has been significantly optimized, the proportion of trade in services has increased year by year, and trade in services and trade in goods have been developing together. (2) Trade in goods has shifted from being export-oriented to paying equal attention to export and import, and the import scale has been expanding. (3) Outbound investment has increased rapidly and even exceeded capital inflows, and the capital flows involve both outflows and inflows. (4) A good pattern of coordinated development between coastal and inland areas has been formed. (5) China's global economic status has been significantly enhanced, and China has actively participated in and even led the formation of international trade and investment rules, playing the role of rule-maker for the world economy.

Post-reading questions:

(1) What did Zhang Qian, the envoy of the Western Han Dynasty, bring back when he returned from Western regions?

(2) Which period in ancient China witnessed the development of the port of Quanzhou?

(3) What is the relationship between a country's foreign trade and people's daily life?

Introduction to Trade Fairs

A trade fair (trade show, trade exhibition or expo) is an exhibition through which companies in a specific industry can showcase and demonstrate their latest products, service, study activities of rivals and examine recent market trends and opportunities. Some trade fairs are open to the public, while others can only be attended by company representatives (members of the trade, e.g. professionals) and members of the press. Therefore, trade shows are classified as either "Public" or "Trade Only". One example is the Frankfurt Book Fair, which is trade-only for its first three days and open to the general public on its final two days. They are held on a continuing basis in virtually all markets and normally attract companies from around the globe.

Trade fairs often involve a considerable marketing investment by participating companies. Costs may include space rental, design and construction of trade show displays, telecommunications and networking, travel, accommodations, and promotional literature and items to give to attendees. In addition, costs are incurred at the show for services such as electrical work, booth cleaning, internet services, and drayage (also known as material delivery). Consequently, cities often promote trade shows as a means of economic development.

1.2.1 Leading Trade Fairs

An increasing number of trade fairs appear online, which are called virtual trade shows. They are gaining in popularity due to their relatively low cost and the convenience of attending or exhibiting without the need for travel. At present, leading trade fairs in China are China Import and Export Fair, China International Import Expo, China Hi-tech Fair and etc.

1.2.1.1 China Import and Export Fair (Canton Fair)

Founded in 1957 by the Ministry of Commerce and Guangdong Provincial Government, China's famous exhibition is a comprehensive international trade event with the longest history, the largest scale, the widest range of commodities, the largest number of purchasers, the widest distribution of countries and regions, the best transaction effect and the best reputation. After years of development, the Canton Fair has become the No.1 promotion platform for China's foreign trade, known as the barometer and weathervane of China's foreign trade, and a window, epitome and symbol of China's opening-up.

1.2.1.2 China International Import Expo (CIIE)

Sponsored by the Ministry of Commerce of the People's Republic of China and The Shanghai Municipal People's Government and undertaken by The China International Import Expo Bureau and the National Convention and Exhibition Center (Shanghai), CIIE is the world's first national-level exhibition with import as the theme.

1.2.1.3 China Hi-tech Fair

The largest and most influential science and technology exhibition in China is jointly organized by the Ministry of Commerce, the Ministry of Science and Technology, the Ministry of Industry and Information Technology, the National Development and Reform Commission, the Ministry of Agriculture and Rural Affairs, the State Intellectual Property Office, the Chinese Academy of Sciences, the Chinese Academy of Engineering and other ministries and commissions and the Shenzhen Municipal Government. It is held annually in Shenzhen. CHTF integrates fruit trading, product exhibition, project investment promotion, cooperation and exchange, and high-level forum, focusing on the display of advanced technologies and products in high-end equipment manufacturing, new energy, new materials, new energy vehicles, energy conservation and environmental protection, and new-generation information technology.

1.2.2 Selecting Trade Fairs

What kind of trade fair or trade show should we attend? Often it is a mix of consumer shows, industry shows, buyers' expositions and educational conferences. Each kind of trade fair has its place. Then let's look at these key factors to decide which trade show is best suited for one's business.

1.2.2.1 Does the Trade Fair Help Meet Your Marketing Goals?

If you are interested in a regional market or new to trade fairs, consider participating in a smaller, local trade fair. If your goal is to acquire the largest number of qualified leads, to support a major new product launch and/or to significantly build awareness, participate in the major industry trade fairs that capture the largest number of target customers. If your objective is to build your network and to position your company as a thought leader, then investigate where your company can be a show's sponsor and your company's representative can be a featured speaker.

1.2.2.2 Is It the Right Market Space?

A trade fair that matches your exact market space is often the best show to attend. You can learn a lot by looking at who exhibits at the possible shows. A list of past exhibitors is usually available from the trade fair management or on their website. Call a few of the past exhibitors and ask about the quality and number of attendees at previous years' shows. Identify the fairs that have an exhibitor attracting your target customers and that are complementary to your business.

1.2.2.3 Determine Which Trade Fairs Your Top Prospects Attend

See if the attendee list from the past fairs is available. Review the list to determine which trade fairs have a large number of your target customers on the attendee list.

1.2.2.4 Identify Which Trade Fairs Your Best Customers Attend

Call your customers and ask which shows they plan to attend and which shows they would like to attend. If there is a show that some of your customers would like to attend but are not planning to attend, ask if they would attend if they received a free pass to the exhibits.

Most major trade shows offer exhibitors a limited number of free passes, so if your customers would attend the show with free passes, this could be a good reason to attend this show.

1.2.2.5 Figure Out Where Your Competition Will Be

How many of your competitors will be exhibiting at the show? If you are not there, will you be at a competitive disadvantage? Trade fairs usually bring together many competitors under one roof. Look for shows where your company will stand out as a leader in your market.

1.2.2.6 Are There Any Special PR Opportunities?

Exhibitors have a distinct advantage of capturing Trade Show PR because they have higher-profiles than attendees. They can also more easily and effectively demonstrate their products. This is particularly important for new product introductions. Ask the Trade Show management for last year's press list and if they have any information on who is planning to cover this year's event. Are there any media outlets attending that provide opportunities for you to reach your target audience in an influential way?

1.2.3 Preparing for a Trade Fair

On the face of it, the task of preparing for attending a trade fair seems overwhelming. The participant has to select a site, negotiate contracts and arrange for booth designing and personnel training as needed. The following are a few steps to follow in preparing for a trade fair:

1.2.3.1 Budgeting

Budget planning is part of the careful preparation for trade fair participation. In addition to basic costs such as stand rental and energy supply, costs may include the cost of designing, constructing and furnishing stands, transportation as well as personnel and travel costs.

1.2.3.2 Setting Up a Goal

As trade show attendees, you are supposed to set up your goal of attending the trade fair. You may build a new mailing list, introduce new product, enhance corporate image, meet new customers, get sales leads, research your market, make direct sales, sign up dealers or distributors, and establish a new position for your company in the industry.

1.2.3.3 Designing the Stand

Trade fair stand is like a company's business card, so it should appeal to the eyes and ears of the customers. Please concentrate on presenting your company most positively when designing your fair stand. Give consideration to company logo, colors, styles, advertising theme, and booth design. The way your booth looks reflects your opinion of your company's position in the marketplace.

1.2.3.4 Recruiting Stand Personnel

Competent stand personnel ensures the success of trade fair participation. The more motivated and qualified the exhibitor's stand personnel is, the greater the opportunities are for good sales results and new contacts. A targeted selection and intensive training of the stand personnel is just as important as an effective presentation of the products. Accordingly, choose people who have knowledge of your product and can convey or demonstrate effectively. Always keep in mind that personalities and "Team Spirits" are important in shaping personnel.

1.2.4 Behaving Properly in Trade Fairs

It is essential that all members of the team should be aware of acceptable behaviors, and unacceptable behaviors when participating in a trade fair. Here are a few guidelines to help you behave in a proper manner in trade fairs.

1.2.4.1 Proper Attire

Proper business attire is essential for conveying an air of professionalism, self-confidence, respectability and competency in the business you are in. It creates a favorable impression on customers and clients, and influences them to do business with you.

For men, it is more appropriate that you wear conservative 2-piece dark suits. The favored color may be navy blue or medium to dark gray. Long sleeved blue or white shirt companies with silk tie complementing in color or style. Black ankle socks, dark polished shoes and matching belt are considered safe accessories.

For women, dark conservative suits may make you appear more professional. The alternative is two piece 1 or 2 button jacket and knee length skirt. To match the suits, you may choose white or light-colored long-sleeved blouse that is not low cut or sheer. Besides that, black well-polished shoes with 1 to 1½ inch heels will be more comfortable when wearing at work. A perfect match of such shoes is a pair of natural tone or sheer black pantyhose.

1.2.4.2 Proper Grooming

It refers to the way of showing and presenting oneself in the trade fair by using cosmetics and makeup tools. It is part of the art of everyday work and a necessary business practice for both men and women.

1.2.4.3 Proper Communication

As booth personnel, presenting skillful conversation tactics is of prime importance. You may address individuals by their titles. You can also enunciate your greeting first. Shake hands correctly with firm eye contact to each customer. If the initial conversation of exchanging information is successful, you may refer to individuals by their names. In this way, further intimate contact may seem possible.

Meanwhile, remain polite and professional when you inquire the visitors to find out if they have good prospects. You may introduce yourself with a one-minute overview of your company and its benefits. Be friendly and polite in inviting: "Let me…", "How about…", "If…, I'd like to…" And then you may talk for another 30 seconds about details on products or services. Afterwards, send out information to visitors for effective follow-up after the event.

1.2.5　Summary

According to a report conducted by Exhibit Source Inc., the average attendee spends 8.3 hours viewing trade show exhibits at a show or fair. That gives you plenty of opportunity to connect with your target audience, consequently, the top three goals for exhibitors at trade fairs are brand awareness, lead generation, and relationship building. As stated by B. Bader, "It takes years sometimes to build a customer relationship—it can take but a moment to destroy it. We never get a second chance to make a first impression." Trade fairs are one arena in which poor etiquette can have negative effects. Mutual trust and clear communication are results of proper etiquette in trade fairs and exhibitions. They promote corporate image, attract new clients and may generate potential business opportunities.

Post-reading Questions:

(4) How should a company prepare to attend a trade fair?

(5) Please search online to find out what sort of behaviors should be avoided for trade show personnel?

Words and Expressions

dynasty	王朝，朝代
maritime	航海的，海事的
envoy	使者，使节，（谈判等的）代表
feudal	封建（制度）的
imperial	帝国的，皇帝的
navigation	航海，航空
tributary	朝贡的
Opium War	鸦片战争
semi-colonial	半殖民地的
Belt and Road Initiative	"一带一路"倡议
business etiquette	商务礼仪
manual	手册
courtesy	礼貌，礼节

virtual trade show	虚拟展会
social norm	社会规范
product assortment	产品组合
affront	侮辱，冒犯
trading delegation	贸易代表团
skill-set	技能组
commodity inspection	商品检验
rapport	融洽，和谐的关系
sponsor	赞助者，主办者
top-notch	顶级
target customer	目标客户
jargon	术语
PR(Public Relation)	公共关系
civilization	文明，文化
potential vendor	潜在供应商
accumulation	聚集，累积
budget	经费，预算
intrinsic	本质的，内在的
allocate	分配
exemplify	例证
stand	展位
stifle	窒息
booth design	展台设计
trade fair/show; exhibition	会展
personnel	工作人员
showcase; demonstrate	展示
business attire	商务着装
telecommunication	电讯，通信
professionalism	专业水平
networking	网络
proper grooming	适当的妆容
accommodation	住宿
cosmetics; makeup	化妆品
promotional literature	宣传资料
conversation tactics	谈话技巧
drayage	短途运输
nametag	名牌
exhibitor	参展商
corporate image	企业形象

Sentences

1. Costs may include space rental, design and construction of trade show displays, telecommunications and networking, travel, accommodations, and promotional literature and items to give to attendees.

费用可能包括场地租金、设计和建造贸易展览展示、电信和网络、旅行、住宿、宣传资料和赠送给与会者的物品。

2. If your goal is to acquire the largest number of qualified leads, to support a major new product launch and/or to significantly build awareness, participate in the major industry trade shows that capture the largest number of target customers.

如果你的目标是获得最多的合格的潜在客户，支持一个主要的新产品的发布和/（或）显著地建立知名度，请参加主要的工业贸易展会，抓住最大数量的目标客户。

3. Budget planning is part of the careful preparation for trade fair participation. In addition to basic costs such as stand rental and energy supply, costs may include the cost of designing, constructing and furnishing stands, transportation as well as personnel and travel costs.

经费预算是为参加贸易展览会所做的精心准备的一部分。除了展台租金和能源供应等基本费用外，费用还包括设计、建造和装备展台、运输以及人员和旅费。

4. Concentrate on presenting your company most positively. Give consideration to company logo, colors, styles, advertising theme, and booth design.

专注于最积极地展示你的公司。特别关注公司标志、颜色、类型风格、广告主题和摊位设计。

5. Proper business attire is essential for conveying an air of professionalism, self-confidence, respectability and competency in the business you are in.

在你所从事的行业中，得体的商务着装对于传达专业、自信、体面和胜任的氛围至关重要。

6. For men, it is more appropriate that you wear conservative 2-piece dark suits, the favored color may be navy blue or medium to dark gray.

对于男性来说，更适合穿保守的两件套深色西装，最适合的颜色可能是海军蓝或中到深灰色。

7. Besides that, black well-polished shoes with 1 to 1½ inch heels will be more comfortable when wearing at work. A perfect match of such shoes is a pair of natural tone or sheer black pantyhose.

除此之外，当你穿着鞋子工作时，黑色擦得闪亮的，鞋跟高度为1至1.5英寸的高跟鞋会更舒服。这种鞋的完美搭配是一双自然色调或纯黑色的连裤袜。

8. You may address individuals by their titles. You can also enunciate your greeting first. Shake hands correctly with firm eye contact to each customer.

你可以称呼别人的头衔。你也可以先清晰地表达你的问候。与每位顾客保持正确的握手姿势和坚定的目光接触。

9. Don't neglect to rehearse your sales message. Consistent message delivery is essential to success.

不要忘记背诵你的销售信息。一致的信息传递是成功的关键。

10. That gives you plenty of opportunity to connect with your target audience, consequently, the top three goals for exhibitors at trade shows are brand awareness, potential customer exploring, and relationship building.

这给了你很多机会与你的目标观众联系，因此，参展商在贸易展会上的三大目标是品牌知名度、开发潜在客户和关系建立。

China International Agricultural Products Fair

China International Agricultural Products Fair (hereinafter referred to as the Fair) is the only large-scale comprehensive agricultural event sponsored by the Ministry of Agriculture and mainly guided and supported by the Ministry of Commerce. It plays an important role in publicizing agricultural policies, displaying agricultural achievements, promoting agricultural technologies, activating the circulation of agricultural products and promoting trade cooperation. It has made a positive contribution to ensuring the supply of agricultural products, promoting farmers' income increase and developing agricultural and rural economy.

On November 27, 2020, the 18th China International Agricultural Products Fair, co-organized by the Ministry of Agriculture and Rural Affairs and Chongqing Municipal People's Government, opened in Chongqing, attracting more than 40,000 professionals from all over the country. As the largest exhibition with the largest number of exhibitors and purchasers and the most comprehensive exhibition categories in the history of the Agricultural Fair, the exhibition is guided by the principle of "Strengthening agriculture with brand, consolidating poverty alleviation achievements". Under the theme of opening up and cooperation for a moderately prosperous society in all respects, the exhibition and sales of poverty alleviation achievements would be strengthened, and new forms and products of agricultural industries world be showcased. The exhibition lasted for four days, and the exhibition area exceeded 200,000 square meters for the first time, which was divided into public welfare exhibition area and market-oriented exhibition area. A series of key events including the Sustainable Development Forum of featured industries in poverty alleviation areas, three special activities for brand promotion of national agricultural enterprises, Digital Rural Development Forum, Agricultural Investment Risk and Social Capital Support for "Agriculture, Rural Areas and Farmers" development Forum, and brand promotion of National Geographical Indications of agricultural products were held.

Questions:

(1) How can China International Agricultural Products Fair help to promote agricultural and rural economy?

(2) What are the highlights of the 18th China International Agricultural Products Fair?

CIIE Key Channel for Global Trade Cooperation

A total of 120,000 cans of pine nuts from Afghanistan, along with a dazzling array of imported products from over 20 countries and regions, were sold out within minutes in livestreams at the ongoing fourth China International Import Expo in Shanghai.

While the small pine nuts whetted the appetite of Chinese consumers, they also offered a vivid example of how China facilitates trade and drives economic development globally, especially for developing countries, industry experts said on Monday.

On Saturday night, e-commerce livestreamers partnered with anchors from CCTV and Xinhua News Agency to conduct several special livestreaming sessions, selling imported goods from 20 countries and regions including Indonesia, South Africa, Serbia and Slovenia.

Livestreaming data showed that the turnover of Afghan pine nuts hit more than 10 million yuan ($1.56 million). The Afghan pine nuts were part of the 45 metric tons of pine nuts that arrived at Shanghai from Kabul earlier this month. This also is the first time that Afghanistan has exported goods to China under the new Taliban-led government.

"It vividly showed that China, with its huge market size and economic vitality, has brought broad development opportunities for countries worldwide, especially for developing countries," said Zhou Mi, a senior researcher at the Chinese Academy of International Trade and Economic Cooperation.

"The stable development of the Chinese market is not only to achieve the country's own development goals, but also can create more value for the international community," Zhou said.

Up to 90 companies from the world's least-developed countries and 600 companies from countries and regions participating in the Belt and Road Initiative have participated in the CIIE this year, said Sun Chenghai, deputy director of the CIIE Bureau.

During this year's mega event, State Development and Investment Corp has signed import contracts with 19 foreign companies for a record $1 billion in total. The company has purchased commodities including barley, cotton, manganese ore and edible oils from 15 economies including Ukraine, Argentina, Russia, Benin and Uruguay.

In addition, through the CIIE, the company has signed a total of $3.47 billion in intent-to-purchase agreements with foreign countries over the past four years, covering cotton, oil and mineral resources. Among them, orders with BRI markets hit $1.91 billion.

"In recent years, the company's trade cooperation with foreign counterparts has expanded to a larger scope and a depper leavel," said Yang Xiaohui, SDIC's deputy general manager.

Visitors looked at jewelry from Oman on Monday at a booth at the China International Import Expo in Shanghai, which closed on Wednesday. Countries involved in the Belt and Road Initiative were displaying their exotic goods at this year's CIIE.

[Source from: CIIE key channel for global trade cooperation—China Economic Net (ce.cn)]

Questions:

(3) In recent years, how did imperters and exporters improve their sales?

(4) Suppose that you are the Chinese liaison of Mr. Will Smith, how could you help him find more business opportunities in China and at the same time, promote regional agricultural products in China?

Zhang Qian's Voyage to the Western Regions

During the War between Chu and Han Dynasties, the Huns seized the chance to expand their power and controlled the vast areas in the northeast, north and west of China. Taking the Western Regions as their military stronghold and economic backing, the Huns also occupied the territory of the Han Dynasty and harassed and pillaged the people of the Central Plains. After Emperor Wu of Han came to the throne, he learned from the mouth of the surrendered Huns that Darouzhi had the intention of revenge but lacked help, so he decided to strengthen the contact with the Western Regions and united with Darouzhi to attack the Huns.

In the second year of Jianyuan (139 BC), Zhang Qian led a team of more than 100 people, with Tang Yifu from the Huns as the guide, set out from Chang'an for the Western Regions and headed west into the Hexi Corridor. When Zhang Qian and his entourages hurried through the Hexi Corridor, they encountered the horsemen of Huns and were all captured, detained and put under house arrest. At the beginning of the third year of Yuanshuo (126 BC), a civil war broke out among the Huns over the throne. Zhang Qian took the opportunity to flee back to Chang'an with Tang Yifu. The journey took 13 years. The whole team consisted of more than 100 people when they set out, but only Zhang Qian and Tang Yifu finally returned.

In the fourth year of Yuanshou (119 BC), Emperor Wu of the Han Dynasty once again sent Zhang Qian to the Western Regions with more than 300 followers, carrying a considerable quantity of gold coins, silk and other goods, as well as 10,000 heads of cattle and sheep. The purpose of this trip was twofold: one was to persuade Wusun people, who were in conflict with the Huns, to return to their hometown in the east and cut off their support to the Huns; the other was to propagandize the power of the Han Dynasty and persuade the states in the Western Regions to unite with the Han Dynasty and attach themselves to the Han Dynasty. When Zhang Qian arrived in Wusun, the country was in turmoil, so he failed to achieve his goal of persuading Wusun to return to the east. However, Zhang Qian's deputy envoys visited the central Asian states of Dayuan, Kangju, Darouzhi and Daxia respectively, expanding the political influence of the Western Han Dynasty and enhancing mutual understanding. Since then, the Han Dynasty and other countries in the Western Regions frequently sent envoys to each other, ranging from a hundred to several hundred. This promoted the development of bilateral trade, and formed a scene of "merchants and vendors and the people from northern tribes were entertained at the frontier region every day".

Questions:

(5) How many times was Zhangqian sent to West Regions?

(6) What was the main purpose of Zhangqian's first trip to West Regions?

Belt and Road Initiative Bridges the Gap between the East and the West

The nation of Georgia hopes to become a logistics hub between Europe and Asia within the framework of the Belt and Road Initiative, a senior Georgian diplomat said in an exclusive interview.

The country's strategic location at the continental crossroads enables it to play an increasingly important role in bridging the Eastern and Western markets, David Aptsiauri, Georgian ambassador to China, said on Wednesday.

"The Belt and Road Initiative has increased the importance of my country," Aptsiauri commented, "Georgia's goal of becoming a logistics hub had added synergy with the initiative."

China and Georgia signed the Memorandum on Silk Road Economic Belt Cooperation in March 2015. The two countries are working on an agreement on international road and rail transportation of passengers and goods, which is hoped to facilitate the development of links between them along the Silk Road.

"The resources of China and other countries involved in the initiative will provide increasing opportunities for development to Georgia", Aptsiauri said. Cooperation between Georgia and China within the initiative framework is "full-fledged", he said. In the past, the bilateral cooperation focused on construction, real estate, trade and energy, he added. "Now we have transportation, logistics, communication, agriculture, banking, tourism and many others, so the range of new fields of cooperation has been expanded."

"Georgia is the first country in Eurasia to have a free-trade agreement with both the European Union and China," Aptsiauri said, "which is beneficial for Chinese companies in terms of easy and low-cost access to regional and international markets."

Aptsiauri praising the relationship between Georgia and China is a good example of how countries of different sizes, resources and cultural aspects can create positive partnerships.

He quoted Georgian experts as saying exports from Georgia to China are expected to increase by 9% and Georgia's imports from China by 2% in two years. "The figures are not so important. The significance is the willingness of the two countries to create favorable conditions for trade relations," Aptsiauri said, "This is also an indication of the willingness of the two countries to support a liberal and open trade policy without barriers."

He said China-Georgia relations are "dynamic" and "oriented towards the long term".

Questions:

(7) What is the new role of Georgia after it joined in "the Belt and Road Initiative"?

(8) What will Georgia benefit from "the Belt and Road Initiative"? What is the future perspective of the relations between China and Georgia?

I. Choose the best answer.

Directions: Please select the best answers from the following four choices.

1. A trade fair is an exhibition organized so that companies in a specific industry can _____.

   A. showcase and demonstrate their latest products and services

   B. meet with industry partners and customers

   C. study activities of rivals, and examine recent market trends and opportunities

   D. all the above

2. What is the overall success of a trade fair?

   A. Etiquette.   B. Brand influence.

   C. Product and service.   D. Business opportunities.

3. If you want to train your booth personnel trade show etiquette, you may consider the following EXCEPT FOR_____.

   A. proper attire and decent appearance

   B. effective business communication skills

   C. booth rental fee

   D. booth personnel skills

4. Why is proper business attire significant to business people?

   A. Because one is regarded as the executive officer when he/she is wearing business attire.

   B. Because of more business opportunities.

   C. Because of high social status.

   D. Because it conveys an air of professionalism, self-confidence, respectability and competency in the business you are in. It creates a favorable impression for customers and clients, and influences them to do business with you.

5. What color is considered safe in business world?

   A. Purple.   B. Black.   C. Light yellow.   D. Gold.

6. What does conservative suit mean to a lady who attends a trade fair?

   A. White T-shirt with jeans.

   B. White shirt with black mini-skirt.

C. Two piece 1 or 2 button jacket and knee length skirt.

D. Sports wear.

7. How can we greet visitors to our booth?

   A. Address them with their honorific or title.

   B. Shake hands correctly and make eye contact.

   C. Use courteous words in greeting, exchanging information and expressing your gratitude.

   D. All the above.

8. If you were a male booth representative, what accessory is needed to bring to a trade exhibition?

   A. Golden ring.   B. Jade bracelet.

   C. Platinum necklace.   D. Watch.

9. What is the synonym for "booth"?

   A. Box.   B. Cube.   C. Stand.   D. Counter.

10. Which of the following is considered unacceptable behavior in a trade show?

    A. Introduce your company and its current profits to potential customers.

    B. Practice and rehearse your sales messages.

    C. Plan to work for your booth schedule.

    D. Block the entrance to your booth.

II. Translation.

Part One

Direction: Translate the following sentences into Chinese.

1. As the world's second largest economy, China is in the middle of a major economic transformation shifting from speed to quality.

2. Last month in Boao, President Xi Jinping unveiled a series of measures to further open up China's economy, including increasing imports and lowering tariffs.

3. With increasing overseas brand penetration and an ongoing online shopping boom, cross-border e-commerce has surged over the past few years and is assuming an increasing role in China's total import and export market.

4. Proposed by China in 2013, the Belt and Road Initiative aims to build trade and infrastructure networks connecting Asia with Europe and Africa along the ancient Silk Road routes.

5. Shaanxi, located in Northwest China, has enjoyed an increasingly important presence on the world stage as an information and logistics hub since the implementation of the Belt and Road Initiative, which calls for global trade and cooperation.

Part Two

Direction: Translate the following dialogue into English.

A：欢迎光临我们的展位。这是我的名片。

B: 谢谢。我想看看你们展示的银耳产品，是哪儿生产的？

A: 谢谢您对我们的产品感兴趣，这是我们最好的产品。我们的公司在福建省古田县，有着多年的银耳培育史和深加工技术。我们的产品是中国国家地理标志产品。

B: 明白了。这些饮料和休闲食品看起来让人食欲大增啊！包装也很精美。

A: 我很开心您喜欢我们的产品。这个系列是我们最好最流行的产品之一，我们手头上有很多来自国内外的询价。我们有专门的介绍，这是产品目录，请过目。

B: 我喜欢这些饮料和零食。这儿还有保健食品，还有面膜和护肤霜呀！

A: 是的，除了银耳粥，我们还有银耳蜂蜜茶、银耳袋泡茶、银耳果冻、银耳酒、银耳面膜、银耳护肤霜，还有银耳孢糖胶囊、银耳降脂胶囊等。产品行销海内外。

B: 价格是多少？

A: 我们的价格是很有竞争力的。我们向您报最优惠价，按此价我们已与其他客户做了大批生意。

B: 很好。下午你在这儿吗？

A: 当然在。

B: 今天下午我会来这儿。

A: 下午见。

B: 再见。

Ⅲ. Fill in the blanks with appropriate word forms.

1. The fancy store provides a wide _____ (assort) of gifts to choose from.

2. The international conference was attended by _____ (delegation) from 56 countries.

3. We were impressed by the _____ (profession) of the staff working at the show.

4. That tragedy gave us the opportunity to look objectively at the goods we'd _____ (accumulation).

5. Kintex is a convention and _____ (exhibit) center located in Gyeonggi Province.

6. All our projects aim to _____ (promotion) the development of poor and remote communities.

7. A survey of retired people has _____ (indicate) that most are independent and enjoying life.

8. The same is true for new technologies for _____ (alleviate) fossil fuel emissions.

9. President Xi Jinping has proposed a road map for The Belt and Road _____ (initial), where he provided a comprehensive vision of how it could contribute to the world development in general.

10. Pack ice around Iceland was becoming a threat to _____ (navigate).

Ⅳ. Extensive reading.

Nine Trends of China's Agricultural Development

Agriculture is the oldest industry, and China has been based on agriculture since ancient times.

As a big agricultural country, China has always put agricultural development in the first place.

Through continuous efforts, China's agriculture has achieved good results in recent years. Food production has achieved unparalleled "eleventh consecutive increase" and farmers' income has increased "eleventh consecutive fast".

However, there are hidden worries behind the gorgeous and high-yielding data. The congenital deficiency of agriculture in China is becoming more and more obvious. At the same time, the situation of Chinese agriculture depending on the weather has not changed fundamentally. Land output rate, resource utilization rate, and labor productivity are low. Meanwhile, the progress of intensive and sustainable development is slow, while various pressures accumulate day by day, which makes agricultural development face unprecedented challenges.

Faced with challenges, only by understanding trends can we win the future.

In the future, what trends and directions will China's agriculture show? Some predictions are discussed as follows:

Scaled agriculture

All along, the agricultural production in China is dominated by small-scale farmers, with, low efficiency and high cost.

In the future, with the improvement of agricultural mechanization level, the trend of agricultural scale will also be strengthened.

Zhang Ziyu, a special commentator of China's Rural Voice, said that the transformation and upgrading of agricultural production requires the main body of operation and the mode of production change from quantity to quality. Rural land transfer has brought new vitality to agriculture.

According to the latest data released by the Ministry of Agriculture, by June of 2016, the total area of contracted cultivated land in China had reached 460 million mu①, which exceeded one third of the total area of contracted cultivated land. These data are telling us that in the future, moderate scale management of agriculture will become an irresistible trend.

New agricultural subject

Compared with the traditional small-scale, self-sufficient and semi-self-sufficient farmer household management, the new type of agricultural management subject was put forward. It usually refers to farmers' professional cooperatives, family farms, major farmers, leading agricultural enterprises and new farmers.

According to the relevant data, up to now, the number of family farms, farmers' cooperatives and other new subjects in China has exceeded 2.7 million.

Experts believe that different types of new agricultural management entities play different roles in the practice of agricultural production and development. Deepening the division of labor among the main bodies will contribute to the realization of economies of

---

① mu, Chinese ancient unit of area. 1mu ≈ 0.0667hm².

scale and the improvement of labor productivity, thus creating more value.

As the object of vigorous support from the state and the backbone of Chinese agriculture, the leading role of the new agricultural management body will be strengthened in the future.

"Internet+agriculture"

At present, China's economic development has entered a new normal. Agricultural development is facing new challenges such as capping the price of agricultural products, raising the cost of production and intensifying the "hard constraint" of resources and environment.

In order to change the mode of agricultural development, "Internet+agriculture" has been put on the agenda of development. Through the use of modern information technology, we can continuously improve the level of agricultural production, management and service, and promote the transformation of agricultural production mode and marketing mode, so as to achieve the production and marketing of agricultural products.

In the future, with the full popularity of the Internet, the application of Internet in the agricultural field will be more extensive, and "Internet+agriculture" will achieve remarkable results.

High-technology agriculture

The impetus of science and technology to modern agriculture is very obvious. In the future, agricultural development should be highly automated and accurate. All environmental control plant factories, the automatic air circulation system, the semi-automatic harvesting system, agricultural robots, agricultural UAVs and so on are the products of high-tech agriculture. In the next one or two decades, with the continuous development of economic globalization and knowledge economy, high technology represented by biotechnology and information technology will continue to infiltrate and integrate into the field of agricultural science and technology. Finally, molecular breeding technology, genetically modified technology, digital agriculture technology, water-saving agriculture technology, food processing technology, space breeding technology and other agricultural high-tech systems will be booming.

Processing of agricultural products

At present, China's agricultural products processing industry, especially the deep processing of agricultural products, is seriously lagging behind, which has become a major bottleneck in the development of agriculture in China.

Breaking through this bottleneck is the basis of accelerating the development of agriculture in China. Agricultural products processing industry is generally some local products or superior agricultural products, scattered raw materials, low technology content, the need for large labor force, for small and medium-sized township enterprises is most suitable.

At the same time, it can also increase employment. From these advantages, the future of agricultural products processing is promising. Moreover, the deep processing of agricultural products will help to increase the added value of products and maximize the benefits of products. It has to be said that the processing of agricultural products is really promising.

Agricultural cultural travel

In recent years, policies to encourage and support the development of Agricultural Cultural tourism have emerged in an endless stream from the state to the local level, and various subsidies have continued to increase. The vane of the policy has pointed out the direction for the development of Agricultural Cultural tourism.

Land use policy will be further preferential, such as encouraging the use of collective construction land in the village to develop leisure agriculture, and renovate idle residential land and surplus construction land for leisure agriculture.

Financial credit support has been further increased. We will guide banking financial institutions to actively explore financing methods such as greenhouse mortgage, forest right mortgage, agricultural machinery mortgage, beach use right mortgage, cash flow mortgage and direct subsidy fund guarantee to meet the diversified financing needs of leisure agriculture development.

Subsidies will continue to grow. In the next five years, subsidy funds for leisure agriculture will continue to grow, and the amount is huge. Find the right department, find the right policy, apply in time, and accurately describe the type of their projects, in order to get rid of the dilemma of inaccessible subsidies.

In the light of national policies, cultural tourism in agriculture will become a major development trend in the future.

Brand in Chinese agriculture

Qu Dongyu, Vice Minister of Agriculture, said that with the acceleration of agricultural modernization, China's agriculture has entered the era of brand.

Brand means prestige and reputation. Brand building and promotion can enhance the added value of agricultural industry and agricultural products, and promote farmers' income.

Nowadays, with the change of the relationship between supply and demand of agricultural products and life styles of consumers, the demand of consumers for agricultural products is no longer the requirement of quality and price, but the higher and higher requirement for the quality of agricultural products.

In the case of serious homogeneity of agricultural products, agricultural enterprises tend to pay too much attention to prices, which will inevitably lead to the continuous decline of competitiveness of enterprises in the long run.

In the future, the competition between agricultural enterprises will no longer be focused on price and quantity, but brand and quality.

Safety of agricultural products

In recent years, the food safety problem of agricultural product has become increasingly prominent, and the quality of agricultural products has been repeatedly questioned.

In view of this phenomenon, the Ministry of Agriculture has accelerated the construction of traceability system of agricultural product quality and safety, and wants to further enhance the supervision ability of agricultural product quality and safety, by implementing the main responsibility of production and operation to enhance the confidence of consumption of edible agricultural products. At the same time, the state vigorously advocates reducing the use of pesticides, chemical fertilizers and other chemicals, and further increasing the safety of agricultural products.

In addition, some agricultural enterprises add two-dimensional codes on their products, so consumers can trace the effective source of products based on this, which greatly increases the safety of agricultural products.

In the future, with the joint efforts of the state, enterprises and consumers, the safety of agricultural products will be guaranteed.

Micro-marketing of agricultural products

Over the years, the cost of traditional agricultural enterprises has been increasing, and e-commerce platform as a new rising power has a marketing strength, but the larger platform fees are relatively high.

As a new platform with almost zero cost, micro-marketing is also a gathering place for new and fashionable people.

Of course, these people are also the main consumer groups. The biggest characteristic of this group is that they are "not leaving their phones", which is known as the "Royal Screen Generation".

Mobile phones and computers are their most frequent means of contacting and interacting with each other on the Internet. Therefore, the marketing of Weibo, Weixin and other means will become a major trend in the future.

China's agriculture has entered a new stage of development, and the era of mass entrepreneurship and innovation has arrived.

If you want to do anything, you can do it. Agriculture is a big market with strong inclusiveness, but the result of mistake and collision must be failure.

Only by grasping the future trend, can we succeed in starting a business!

Please complete the following tasks.

Task 1: True or false statements.

(1) The congenital efficiency of agriculture in China is increasingly obvious. (   )

(2) The transformation and upgrading of agricultural production require the main body of operation and the mode of production change from quality to quantity. (   )

(3) New type of agricultural management subject refers to farmers' professional cooperatives, family farms, major farmers, leading agricultural enterprises and new farmers. (   )

(4) The application of Internet to agriculture may cause brain drain. (   )

(5) High technology represented by geographical science and information technology will continue to infiltrate and integrate into the field of agricultural science and technology. (   )

(6) Farmers may produce only the raw agricultural products to increase the added value of products and maximize the benefits of products. (   )

(7) Brand establishing and promotion can increase the added value of agricultural industry and agricultural products, and promote farmers' income. (   )

(8) Some agricultural enterprises add three-dimensional codes on their products. (   )

(9) As a new platform with almost zero cost, macro-marketing is also a gathering place for X-generation. (   )

(10) Agriculture is a big market with strong exclusiveness. (   )

Task 2: Group discussion and presentation.

Suppose that you and your teammates are officials from Agricultural Bureau of Fujian Province, your mission is to introduce to Mr. Will Smith, our South African friend, the featured agricultural products and advanced marketing channels in Fujian Province, such as edible fungi cultivation and manufacture, as well as e-commerce channels. How would you accomplish the task? Based on the reading material, you may search online for information and prepare a business presentation.

Ⅴ. Writing practice.

Please write a summary of NO MORE THAN 250 words based on the above reading material "Nine Trends of China's Agricultural Development".

Chapter 2 Establishing Business Relations

Task Driven

Founded in 1989, Fujian Mushroom Import & Export Co., Ltd. has grown into an international brand enterprise integrating scientific research, cultivation, production, processing, sales, and cultural inheritance of ganoderma. Jenny Zhang, a sales representative, finds that South Africa Sprout International Corporation has some interest in Reishi mushroom and wants to send an email to establish business relationship with them.

You are required to write a sales letter for Jenny Zhang.

Learning Objectives

• **Knowledge objectives:** Understand the purpose and channels of establishing business relations; Master the principles of drafting a sales letter; Remember the useful expressions of drafting a sales letter.

• **Skill objectives:** Apply 7C principles into drafting a sales letter.

• **Affective objectives:** Grasp the importance of 7C principles in written business communication.

Core Concept

2.1 Purpose of Establishing Business Relations

To establish business relations with prospective dealers is one of the vitally important measures either for a newly established firm or an old one that wishes to seek new customers, to consolidate existing relations, to expand new markets and to enter into new fields of business activities.

The letter for establishing business relations can be a sales letter, also called an initial letter. It is a piece of direct mail designed to persuade the reader, as a potential customer, to purchase a particular product or service in the absence of a salesperson. Sometimes, the importer also can send an initial letter or email to the exporter inviting a quotation.

Channels to Establishing Business Relations

Imagine that you work in a sales department and are required to promote a new product to the company you do not know. Then, what are you going to do?

First, you can obtain the information from Business-to-Business (B2B) platforms. B2B is a transaction or business conducted between one business and another, such as a wholesaler and a retailer. B2B transactions tend to happen in the supply chain, where one company will purchase raw materials from another to be used in the manufacturing process. Meanwhile, B2B transactions are also commonplace for auto industry companies, as well as property management, housekeeping, industrial cleanup companies, and etc.. Some famous B2B platforms are as follows: Alibaba, Global Sources and Made-in-China. Furthermore, the information can be also obtained through the following channels:

(1) Trade fairs and exhibitions;
(2) Banks;
(3) Chamber of Commerce;
(4) Commercial Counselor;
(5) Newspaper, magazine or TV;
(6) Business partners;
(7) Social networking tools: Linked-In, Facebook, and Twitter;
(8) Market research;
(9) Website: search engine or company websites.

Basic Structure of Initial Letter/Email

The initial letter/email should be friendly, simple, and informative in language. Before writing this letter or email, you should take the following questions into consideration:

(1) What is your objective?
(2) Who is your reader?
(3) What kind of presentation should you use?

Meanwhile, the initial letter usually has a basic structure, which is shown as follows:

(1) Indicate the source of information and writing purpose;

(2) Introduce the company and product;
(3) Make a requirement or express your wishes;
(4) End politely.

2.4 Writing Principles

In order to write a trial letter with a response rate of more than 20%, the initial letter must be concise and clear, reflecting mature business thinking and professional skills, which are summarized as follows:

(1) Focus on one or two topics;
(2) State clearly how you get their company's name;
(3) State your purpose directly in the first paragraph;
(4) Introduce the company overview, business scope and comparative advantages of the company concretely and concisely;
(5) Select a proper product to make a specific recommendation;
(6) Name some famous clients;
(7) It is not recommended to attach pictures to your initial letter. If you must attach pictures, please control the size within 100K.

Words and Expressions

Quotation/offering price	报价
a quotation sheet	报价单
catalogue/brochure/pamphlet	报价目录
delivery lead time	订货交货周期
a trial order	试订单
best seller	畅销货，大卖
quick-selling product line	快销产品线
long-standing customer	老客户
sample order	样品订单
Chamber of Commerce	商业行会
consumer fair	消费者博览会
buying leads	采购信息，买家信息
selling leads	供应信息，卖家信息
business line(s)	业务范围
yellow book/page	电话薄黄页

collectively-owned enterprise	集体企业
privately-owned enterprise	私营企业
agency	公司、代理行
Messrs	收货人，两位或两位以上男子
public company	上市公司
state-operated corporation	国营公司
state-owned corporation	国有公司
deal in sth.	经营某物
deal with sb.	与某人做生意
specialize in	专营
seek for	寻找，寻求
to our mutual benefit	对双方有利
by courtesy of	承蒙…许可
state-owned private management enterprise	国有民营企业
small and medium-sized enterprises (SMEs)	中小企业
township/rural enterprise	乡镇企业
inquiries are cordially welcomed	欢迎洽购
to enjoy high reputation at home and abroad	誉满国内外
Commercial Counselor's Office	商务参赞处
enter into business relations with sb.	与某方开展业务关系
through the courtesy of	感激某人（单位）的推荐（介绍）
to owe one's name and address to sb.	承蒙某人告知…名称和地址
be in the market for sth.	预购某物
be in a position to do sth.	某人能够做某事
enclosed please find sth. /enclosed is sth.	随函附上
We shall/would appreciate it if sb. would...	如果某人能够…我们将会十分感激
in great need of sth.	大量需求
The market is firm/strong/rising/advancing/soaring	市场行情坚挺
The market is weak/retreating/declining	市场疲软
be within (fall within, come under) the scope of our trade activities	属于我们的经营范围
be within (lie within, fall within) our business scope/sphere	
to establish with sb. long-term economic relations	与某人建立长期的经济联系

Sentences

1. We take the liberty of writing to you with a view to building/entering into/establishing business relations with your firm.

我们冒昧通信，以期与你公司建立业务往来。

2. We are glad to send you this introductory letter, hoping that it will be the prelude to mutually beneficial relations between us.

我们欣然寄发这些自荐信，希望是互利关系的前奏。

3. We have the pleasure to introduce ourselves to you and hope we may cooperate with you in your business extension.

我们很高兴认识贵方，盼望有机会合作，扩展业务。

4. We wish to establish direct negotiation with you with a view to introducing your special lines into our market.

我们希望与贵公司建立业务联系，以便将贵公司的专营品介绍到我们市场。

5. We are a professional exporter of toys in China with more than 10 years' experience and have already set up a long-lasting good reputation in the world market, due to our good management system and excellent after-sales service.

我方具备10多年的经验，是中国专业的玩具出口商。由于良好的管理制度和出色的售后服务，我们已在国际市场上建立了良好的信誉。

6. Your firm has been kindly recommended to us by Messrs. J. Smith & Co., Inc., in New York, as large importers of furniture.

纽约史密斯有限公司向我们推荐，贵公司是家具业的主要进口商。

7. We have obtained your company's name and address through the Commercial Counselor's Office of the Embassy of the People's Republic of China in your country and understand that you would like to establish business relations with us.

我们从贵国的中国大使馆商务参赞处得到贵公司的行名和地址，并获悉，贵公司愿意同我们建立业务关系。

8. From Alibaba.com, we learn that you are a potential buyer of Chinese textiles, which just falls within our business scope.

我方从阿里巴巴网站获悉，贵公司是中国纺织品的潜在买家，而纺织品正属于我们的经营范围。

9. We are exporters with long standing and high reputation engaged in exportation the following articles; the purpose of this letter is to explore the possibilities of developing trade with you.

我们是声誉卓著的出口商，长期经营下列商品的出口业务，本信的目的是探讨与你们发展贸易的可能性。

10. To give you a general idea of the scope of our business activities, we enclose herewith a complete set of catalogues that we are dealing in.

为使您能全面了解本公司的业务范围，随函附上一套我们经营产品的目录。

11. Having many years of constant dealings with the leading manufacturers here, we are confident that we can execute your order at the lowest possible price.

我方与本地大厂商有多年的持续业务往来，所以确信能以最低的价格来执行贵方的订单。

12. You may rest assured that all of our items can be supplied in a wide range of designs

to meet the requirements of a fashion trade such as yours.

贵方尽可放心，我们所有产品均可以各种款式供应，足以满足像贵方这样的时尚行业的需求。

13. With excellent quality, attractive appearance and good price, our products have been winning good sales for more than 20 years in the world market.

由于品质优良、外观漂亮、价格优惠，20多年来我方产品在国际市场上一直有很好的销量。

14. With more than 10 years' experience in handling agricultural products, we not only have many distributors in each area but also have very good direct sales channels.

基于10多年的经营农产品的经验，我们不仅在各地区拥有很多分销商，而且也有很好的直接销售渠道。

15. There is a steady demand in China for high-quality goods of this kind. Sales are not very high, but a very good price can be ensured for fashionable designs.

中国对这种产品的优势品种有稳定的需求，销售量虽不会很大，但流行款式能卖很好的价格。

Case One: A sales letter from the seller

Dear Mr. David Green,

I got your name and company information from google listing. Hope you had a nice weekend. This is Jenny Zhang from Fujian Mushroom Import & Export Co., Ltd. in China.

Founded in 1989, we specialize in rare edible-medicinal fungi products such as Reishi Mushroom. Our plantations and its processed products have been certified organic in China, the US, the EU and Japan.

With certifications such as GLOBAL G.A.P., KOSHER, HALAL and ISO 22000:2005, our products also own the drug production license, the drug GMP certificate, the food production license (including common food and health food), and the export food production enterprise record-keeping certificate. We rank first in exporting organic Reishi products in China.

With a wide range of fungi products, we do have a lot of products which meet your requirements, like the Reishi coffee, Reishi tea and Ganoderma lucidum. Attached are some pictures for your reference.

If you are interested in our products, please feel free to contact me so that I can provide you with more valuable information.

Best regards,

Jenny Zhang
Sales
Fujian Mushroom Import & Export Co., Ltd.
Alibaba.com: Ganoherb Raw
Amazon.com: GANOHERB
Ebay:ganoherb

Case One Analysis

Business practice

It is of crucial importance to do market research and identify prospective clients. There are various channels for the seller to find information about potential clients, such as search engines, B2B platforms, trade fairs, trade directories, chambers of commerce, etc. In this case, Jenny found this client's company name and email address through Google. In order to tap into the market of South Africa, she wrote an email to Mr. Green as a goodwill gesture, aiming to seek a new business opportunity. In writing this kind of emails, the key is to highlight the company's strength and capture the buyer's attention.

Writing strategy

This email is organized as follows:
(1) To mention the source of the buyer's information (company name and email address);
(2) To introduce her company (the company name, business scope, experience in this line, position in the industry, product strength, etc.);
(3) To recommend a few products that may interest the buyer;
(4) To express the wish of receiving a reply from the buyer and show her intention to establish business relations.

Business terms

(1) GLOBAL G.A.P.: The majority of retailers in today's markets require certain standards that ensure safe and sustainable agriculture. GLOBAL G.A.P. certification is highly regarded for demonstrating on-farm food safety and sustainability. By complying with GLOBAL G.A.P. standards, producers can sell their products both locally and globally. The GLOBAL G.A.P.'s main standard, Integrated Farm Assurance, is available for three scopes of production: crops, livestock, and aquaculture.

(2) KOSHER: The Kosher certificate is a document issued by certification agencies and the Chief Rabbinate of Israel, in which a Rabbi certifies that the products referred (usually food products) fulfill the biblical precepts of the Jewish religion. This certificate is not only required for Israel but also for other countries in which there are Jewish communities calling

for kosher products, such as the USA, United Kingdom, France, Russia, Argentina, and Mexico. Kosher certificates are requested especially for food: meat (slaughter of animals and salting process), fish, milk and eggs, canned and preserved foods. They also include feed additives (preservatives and dyes) and fiber of animal origin.

(3) HALAL: Halal certification applies to the food, cosmetic and pharmaceutical sectors and attests that a product is manufactured in full compliance with the precepts of Islamic Law, that it does not include any "forbidden" components, and has in no way been in contact with any substances or objects considered "impure".

(4) (ISO 22000:2005): (ISO 22000:2005) is a company level certification based on a standard published by the International Organization for Standardization (ISO) titled "Food safety management systems-Requirements for any organization in the food chain". The standard is in place to aid organizations in their efforts to control food safety hazards to ensure that food is safe at the time of human consumption. The standard states that an organization should consider the construction and lay-out of facilities, waste disposal, storage and transportation, pest control, sanitation and personnel hygiene when establishing a prerequisite program.

Case Two: An initial letter from the buyer

Dear Sir or Madam,

We are a young company in the food industry focusing on superfoods, which we market via e-commerce in South Africa and even the whole African market. Meanwhile, we have many branches around the world, such as in Japan and South Korea. We got your name from Alibaba and are particularly interested in your Reishi coffee, Reishi tea and Ganoderma lucidum.

We intend to test the market with smaller quantities by marketing new products. After the successful test phase, we will gradually increase our purchase quantities. We also prefer business partners who can supply us with private labeling.

We would be grateful if you could provide us with a quote for your Ganoderma Lucidum and Ganoderma Sinense.

Please provide us with the following information:
- Minimum order quantity for private labeling.
- Payment terms and conditions.

We would be interested in doing business with you, given a workable quote, and potentially increase the variety of goods we purchase from you. Considering the first order, we would be delighted if you could give us your best possible price for these items.

We are looking forward to hearing from you.
Regards,

David Green
Managing Director
South Africa Sprout International Corporation

Case Two Analysis

Business practice

Companies dealing with international trade often promote sales of their products through B2B e-commerce platforms or their own official websites. If potential buyers feel interested in certain items after browsing these websites, they may take the initiative to contact the seller, and seek the possibility of establishing business relationships. In this case, the buyer found the information of the seller through Alibaba website, and wrote to inquire about the price of several articles. In order to get a favorable price from the seller, the buyer described the company's business scope and market condition. He also indicated the possibility of placing more orders if the price would be favorable. In addition, he asked for the information of minimum order quantity and payment terms, which also showed his genuine desire to do business with the seller.

Writing strategy

This email is organized as follows:
(1) To give a brief company introduction (e.g. business scope);
(2) To mention the source of contact information;
(3) To explain the purpose of writing (to find a supplier of new products);
(4) To invite a quote on specific articles from the seller;
(5) To describe the market condition so as to get a good offer;
(6) To express the expectation of a reply.

Pragmatic analysis

Generally speaking, business correspondence can achieve communicative efficiency and effectiveness by following the 7C principles, which include correctness, completeness, concreteness, clarity, conciseness, consideration and courtesy. Let's analyze the features of completeness, concreteness and courtesy through this email. Firstly, each paragraph of this email focuses on one topic, and the whole email contains all the necessary information for building business relationships, which shows the completeness feature of business writing. In this email, the writer described his writing purpose, introduced the company's business scope and market condition, and inquired information about the goods that interested him. Secondly, this email is also characterized by concreteness. The writer mentioned the specific product name (Reishi coffee, Reishi tea and Ganoderma lucidum) and source of information (Alibaba), and inquired information in a concrete manner (e.g. order quantity, payment and price). Lastly, the feature of courtesy is clearly manifested in the wording of this email, as the writer used many emotional expressions and if-clauses to express thanks and joys and to show politeness. The example utterances that display courtesy are "We would be grateful if you could provide", "Please provide" and "we would be delighted if you could give".

I. Choose the best answer.

1. In order to _____ our business to your country, we are writing to you to _____ possibilities of cooperation.
   A. expand, seek   B. seek, expand   C. extend, seek   D. seek, extend

2. We specialize _____ the export of Japanese Light Industrial Products and would like to trade _____ you in this line.
   A. in, in   B. in, with   C. with, in   D. with, with

3. Our mutual understanding and cooperation will certainly _____ important business.
   A. lead to   B. lead from   C. attend to   D. attend on

4. Your firm has been kindly _____ to us by your sister firm.
   A. commented   B. amended   C. recommended   D. commended

5. The purpose of this letter is to _____ the possibilities of developing trade with you.
   A. explain   B. extend   C. explore   D. explode

6. We make you the following offer _____ your reply reaching no later than noon time December 25.
   A. subject to   B. subject for   C. object to   D. object for

7. We are _____ exporters of all kinds of Italian goods.
   A. good-equipped   B. well-established
   C. good-established   D. well-equipped

8. We would be pleased to receive your _____ export prices on the basis of CIF Beijing.
   A. illustrated   B. illustrating   C. explaining   D. explained

9. Our market survey informs us that you are _____ oil pump equipment.
   A. for the market of   B. in the marketplace for
   C. for the marketplace for   D. in the market for

10. We have an inquiry _____ large quantity of walnut meat.
    A. for   B. in   C. at   D. on

II. Translation.

Part One

Direction: Translate the following sentences into Chinese.

1. We have seen your advertisement in the latest issue of "China's Foreign Trade" and are

interested in different kinds of wood fittings.

2. Specializing in the export of Chinese Black Tea, we wish to trade with you in this line.

3. As a leading importer of Aquaculture Equipment in the UK, we have an extensive sales connection and a thorough knowledge of the local market.

4. We wish to introduce ourselves as an exporter of fertilizers with many years' experience.

5. Your firm has been recommended to us by the P. R. C. Consul in your city as a large exporter of Woolen Goods.

Part Two
Direction: Translate the following sentences into English.
6. 我们想借此机会与您建立业务关系。
7. 随附我们的价目表和促销资料供您参考。
8. 如果您能立即寄来产品目录表，我们将不胜感激。
9. 由于良好的质量和合理的价格，我们的产品在全球市场上广受欢迎。
10. 我们经营各种水果罐头，在德国市场享有盛誉。

Ⅲ. Fill in the blanks with appropriate words.

1. We request you to furnish us _____ a full range _____ samples.

2. As this item falls _____ the scope of our business activities, we shall be pleased to enter _____ direct business relations _____ you.

3. Quotations and sample books will be airmailed _____ you _____ receipt of your specific inquiry.

4. We trust that your initial order will be placed _____ us soon.

5. The company has informed us that you are _____ the market _____ silk fabrics.

6. We specialized _____ the exportation of Chinese silk cloth.

7. We have been _____ this line _____ many years.

8. The document will be sent to you _____ your reference.

9. We are sending you this special offer _____ the hope that you will introduce them to other buyers.

10. All the offered prices are net _____ commission.

Ⅳ. Extensive reading.

The Seven "C's" Principles of Writing English Business Letters

There are seven principles which must be observed in writing English business letters. Since all these seven principles are begun with the letter "C", we can call them the "7C's".

Consideration

In preparing for every piece of information and before taking every steps, you must always keep your reader in mind and think about your opposite side. There is an old saying:

"Put yourself in other's shoes." It means that you must always show your consideration for your correspondents.

Courtesy
When writing to your correspondents, it is necessary for you not only to be polite, but also to be sincere, tactful, thoughtful and appreciative. It is also a kind of courtesy for the tradesmen to answer letters the inquiries promptly. Any delay in dealing with the matters is discourteous.

Clarity
The writer should express his aims, ideas and requirements clearly not only by distinct and understandable wordings, but also by correct phrases, tenses, voices and sentence structures in order not to be misunderstood or misinterpreted. Writing letters for enquiring about the same thing will cause you lose business opportunities.

Conciseness
A letter written with wordiness or redundancy will not be welcomed in the business field, which is just like a battle field. The aim of doing business is to gain profits from fighting a quick battle to result in a quick decision in winning over the business opportunities. In writing letters, the sentences you use must be brief and to the point.

Concreteness
The inquiries of others about something and your answers to the others' letters must be made with reality and concreteness. Any ambiguous and vague words must be deleted and the information must be supplied with definiteness and concreteness.

Completeness
The business letters must consist of complete and intact information. The incomplete information will fail to enable the tradesmen to seize the business opportunities of doing mutually beneficial trades.

Correctness
Whenever you are writing letters, faxing or E-mailing, you must check the typing of figures, types, specifications, etc.. Before sending it out, you should check the mail again in order not to make mistakes.

Please complete the following tasks.

Task 1. Rewrite the following sentences to make them concise and effective.
(1) The plant is successful in terms of production.

(2) We wish to acknowledge receipt of your letter of July 5th.

(3) We are informed that similar goods of American origins have been sold here at a level about 30% lower than yours.

(4) He will fly to Germany next week for the purpose of meeting Mr. Stwartz in person.

(5) This product not only is welcomed for its reasonable price, but also for its fine quality.

Task 2. Rewrite the following sentences according to the principle of correctness.
(1) Your demand for a 5% discount off the order of the goods narrows our profit margin and we could not warrant it.

(2) If there are some problems with the bikes, you can return it back to us, even though over the warranty, we will change it without charge.

(3) We'll deliver you some trial orders because of the satisfaction of your price and quality.

(4) As the market is declining, we recommend your immediate acceptance.

Task 3. Rewrite the following sentences according to the principle of consideration.
(1) We are shipping your order on Friday.

(2) Your letter is not clear at all. I can't understand it.

(3) You must complete the enclosed form if you need correct shipment.

(4) Unfortunately, your shipment won't be sent until January 3.

(5) Upon receiving your L/C amendment, we will arrange to have your goods shipped.

V. Writing practice.

Please finish the writing task for establishing business relations and follow the writing tips for a trial letter below.

With the rapid development of various social platforms on the Internet, the content of the trial letter is becoming more and more open. For different customers, you should create a variety of templates for different content, which will be more targeted. In order to write a trial letter with a response rate of more than 20%, the letter must be concise and clear, reflecting mature business thinking and a professional skills as follows:

- Indicating the purpose of the letter and the source of customer information.
- Introducing the company overview, business scope and comparative advantages of the company.
- Having a product introduction. In order to meet the needs of the other party, it is necessary to select a specific product to make a specific recommendation. Otherwise, it can be a general introduction to the overall situation of the company's products, such as quality standards, prices and sales. It is also common to use catalogues, quotations or other samples for reference.
- It is not recommended to attach pictures to your trial letter. If you must attach pictures, please control the size within 100K.
- For targeted sales letters sent to customers, you do not need to read the receipt, it is strongly recommended to add high priority to the mail.
- Don't introduce everything for the first time, as the customer will be very impatient. If there is no reply for the first time, you can send a letter again. When you have a new product, you can also recommend it to your target customer. Sometimes it will pay off if you insist on it.

Chapter 3

Price Negotiation (Enquiry, Offer & Counter-offer)

Task Driven

David Green, General Manager of South Africa Sprout International Corporation, came to China to attend the Fuzhou Agricultural Fair. After the initial communication with the sales representative of Fujian Mushroom Import & Export Co., Ltd. at the exhibition, Mr. Green learned about specialties such as Reishi (ganoderma) and shiitake mushrooms. He also visited the Juncao Research Center after the fair. Please work in groups to practice price negotiation in email writings. The groups will be divided into buyers and sellers, representing Fuzhou and South Africa respectively, to negotiate the price of fungi products. The groups are required to write a set of negotiation emails including establishing business relationship, enquiry, offer and counter-offer. Please highlight the key information such as characteristics of fungi products and payment terms.

Learning Objectives

- **Knowledge objectives:** Understand the definitions and process of enquiry, offer, and counter-offer and their relationship; Recite useful expressions for business negotiations.
- **Skill objectives:** Properly write emails of enquiry, offer and counter-offer.
- **Affective objectives:** Observe rules of international trade by avoiding false enquiry; Seek common ground and achieve a win-win cooperation in business negotiations.

Core Concept

3.1 Enquiry

3.1.1 Defining an Enquiry

An enquiry is a request from the buyer for information on the supply of certain goods without engagement. An enquiry can be made online, by phone, by fax, by letter or e-mail. Traditionally, an enquiry is made almost without exception by the buyer in order to get necessary information about the products, services or information he/she wants to buy, such as price, quality, specifications, etc. Unlike the traditional enquiry, the seller, however, tends to take the initiative to send an enquiry to potential overseas buyers in hopes of developing a new business relationship in today's international business activities.

3.1.2 Classifying the Enquiry

Generally, an enquiry falls into two categories: a general enquiry and a specific enquiry. A general enquiry usually refers to some general information by asking for some brochures, price lists, literature, samples, etc. A specific enquiry indicates that the buyer has an intention to buy a particular product, so they make a detailed enquiry including price terms, specifications, quantity available, payment terms, shipment, insurance, etc. The format of an enquiry letter often includes such elements as self address, date, receiver's address, salutation, subject, body paragraphs, subscription, and enclosure.

3.1.2.1 Structure of General Enquiry

(1) State the source of information;
(2) Indicate the writing purpose;
(3) Introduce the business;
(4) Make some requirements;
(5) End with good wills.

3.1.2.2 Structure of Specific Enquiry

(1) State the specific enquiry including specification, quantity, delivery date, payment terms, insurance, and etc.;
(2) Indicate some requirements;
(3) State the wish for the period of a reply;
(4) End in a polite way.

3.1.3 Judging a Valuable Enquiry

You can decide whether an enquiry is valuable or not by looking into the source of the enquiry, investigating the information about the captioned company, and double checking the content of the enquiry. To be specific, in order to find out how valuable an enquiry is, you can read the subject, find out how the buyer makes an enquiry, have a background research about the customer, analyze the content of enquiry letters, which can be classified into three types: false enquiry, tentative enquiry and valid enquiry. Different from false enquiry or tentative enquiry which always requires for some general information of products, valid enquiry requests for details of a specific product in the seller's product line. Sometimes, the buyer will ask if the seller can produce a specific product not in their product line but similar in manufacturing process, and encloses specifications. Sometimes, the buyer will provide their own sample, asking if the seller can produce it, or offer a quotation for a specific quantity.

3.2 Offer

3.2.1 Defining an Offer

An offer in international business refers to a promise to supply goods on the terms and conditions for the buyer's consideration and acceptance, such as price terms and payment terms. A satisfactory offer includes the name of commodities, quality, unit price and type of currency.

The person who asks for an offer is called offeree, while the one who makes an offer is called the offeror. In modern international business, due to the increasing peer competition, instead of passively waiting for any business opportunities to come, the sellers are inclined to take the initiative to send their catalogue to the prospective buyers abroad by all manner of means in the hope of getting more orders.

3.2.2 Classifying Offers

There are two categories of offers: firm offers and non-firm offers. The firm offer is a contractual obligation. Therefore, once it has been accepted unconditionally within the terms of validity it cannot be withdrawn. A firm offer should be provided with two major requirements. First, in firm offers the seller encloses complete, affirmative, specific terms of business. The major conditions of the contract are required including names of goods, quality specifications, prices, quantity, time of delivery, shipping, terms of payment, packing and insurance. A firm offer features a binding force upon the offeror as he/she cannot refuse to sell the goods to the offeree once he/she makes a firm offer. Besides the time of validity, a firm offer must state distinctly that the offer is firm or irrevocable.

A non-firm offer is a quotation subject to the final confirmation and is not legally binding. The offeror can withdraw it any time before the offeree accepts it. A non-firm offer is also called a free offer which is a proposal made by offeror ready to sell on certain conditions. Unlike a firm offer, a non-firm offer has no binding force on the offeror and offeree. In a non-firm offer the offeror need not state the complete terms of sale and the time of validity.

Counter-offer

3.3.1 Defining a Counter-offer

A counter-offer is a bid from the offeree. To be specific, it is a proposal made by one party to disagree to an offer made by the other. In international trade, if the offeree, the buyer in most cases, disagrees with the offeror, often the seller, for what has been offered to him/her, he/she will come up with a counter-offer for further negotiation. When we make a counter-offer, price is the most important thing that the buyer considers. Also, the buyer will bargain on other aspects such as price terms, payment terms, packing or shipment.

3.3.2 Process of a Counter-offer

When a counter-offer takes place, the role of the two parties will change accordingly. With the counter-offer, the original offeree, or the buyer, now becomes the offeror, while the original offeror, or the seller, becomes the offeree. A reply to an offer, which does not agree with any or some of the terms of the offer, is viewed as a rejection to the offer and becomes a counter-offer. A counter-offer means that the offeree does not accept the offer wholly but comes up with some additions, modifications, or limitations with regard to the terms and conditions included in the offer. Once a counter-offer is made, the original offer by the offeror loses its validity immediately.

Words and Expressions

the subject company	上文提到的公司
the firm concerned	有关商行
business capacity	业务能力

reciprocate	回报，报答
courtesy	恩惠，慷慨
acknowledge	承认，确认
packing	包装
quantity	数量
specifications	规格
shipment	装运，装运的货物
payment	支付（方式）
inquiry	询盘
offer	报盘
firm-offer	实盘
non-firm offer	虚盘
counter-offer	还盘
confirmed	保兑的
irrevocable	不可撤销的
L/C (letter of credit)	信用证
draft	专有名词，指汇票
engagement	正式的承诺或保证
stock	库存
discount	折扣
advise	通知，告知
credit standing/credit reputation	信用状况
inquire for	询价
be well connected with	关系广泛
in the line of…	在…行业中
a ready market	销路好
be of good quality	质量上乘
preferably by…	最好用…
in receipt of	收到
rush sb. samples by airmail	速航寄样品
under separate cover	另封
as requested	按照要求（请求）
in due course	适时
as follows	如下
be subject to…	以…为准（条件）
take please in doing sth.	高兴做某事
provided/provided that	倘若
make/send/give/fax offer for sth.	报…盘
a rise in price	价格上涨
easy care	使用方便

finalize an order　　　　　　　　　　　　完成或达成交易
brisk demand　　　　　　　　　　　　　　不断的需求
grant one's request　　　　　　　　　　　同意…的请求
lower the price　　　　　　　　　　　　　降价
market levels　　　　　　　　　　　　　　市场行情
a growing demand for…　　　　　　　　　对…的需求日益增长

Sentences

1. We enquire for 50,000 pieces of leather shoes.
我方询问5万双皮鞋的价格。

2. This is the rock-bottom price and any further reduction is out of the question.
这是最低价，不能再降价。

3. We have been maintaining an account with them.
我方一直与他们保持账户往来。

4. We have never failed to meet their obligation.
我方从未有过不履行义务的事情。

5. We acknowledge with thanks receipt of your letter.
收到来信，表示感谢。

6. We are well-connected with major dealers in the line of textile.
我们与纺织业的经销商有很好的关系。

7. Please rush us your quotation by fax.
请以传真速寄报价单。

8. The color doesn't agree with my taste.
这颜色不符合我方的品味。

9. We are in receipt of your letter dated May 12th, 2015.
收到贵方2015年5月12日来信。

10. Please make us an offer for leather shoes.
请给我方报皮鞋盘。

11. If you accept our offer, please fax us your confirmation.
如果贵方接受我方的报盘，请电传我方表示确认。

12. Chinese leather shoes always find a ready market in North America.
中国皮鞋在北美地区市场的销路一直很好。

13. It will be appreciated, if you let us have your best firm offer.
如蒙报给我方最好的实盘，我方将不胜感激。

14. We wish to confirm our fax dispatched on July 6th about the offer without engagement the following.
现确认7月6日传真不受约束盘如下。

15. Your inquiry is having our immediate attention and we hope to make you an acceptable offer in a few days.
我方正在研究贵方询盘，几天内便可给贵方合适的报盘。

16. We thank you for your enquiry on Nov.19th and are sending you, under a separate cover, a sample of leather shoes together with our price list.

感谢贵方于 11 月 19 日询盘，现另封寄上皮鞋样品及价目单。

17. We confirm having faxed you a firm offer for the following goods subject to your reply reaching us by September 25th.

确认已向贵方电开下述商品实盘，9 月 25 日前有效。

18. We regret to say that we cannot entertain the offer you sent us 5 days ago.

很抱歉，我们对你方 5 天前发来的报盘不予考虑。

19. If your price is competitive, we would like to place an order with you.

如果贵方价格具有竞争性，我们将愿意与你们下订单。

20. There is no possibility of our cutting the price to the extent you indicated.

把价格降低到贵方所提出的水平是不可能的。

21. Although your price is below our level, we accept, as an exception, your order with a view to initiating business with you.

贵方价格低于我们的水平，但为开展业务，我方破例接受贵方价格。

22. We are anticipating with keen interest your favorable reply.

我们盼望贵方肯定的答复。

23. We shall inform/advise you of the name of the ressel and the date of sailing.

我方将告知贵方船名和起航日期。

24. Please send us your best offer by fax indicating origin, packing, detailed specifications, quantity available and the earliest time of shipment.

请以传真报最优惠盘，并注明原产地、包装、详细规格、可供数量及最早装运时间。

Case One: Enquiry

Dear Ms. Jenny Lin,

Thanks for your interest in establishing business relationship with us.

We are a young company in the food industry focusing on superfoods, which we market via e-commerce in South Africa, Japan and other countries. After visiting your Alibaba shop, we find that your products may well fall into our scope, which has a potential market in Japan.

We have heard about the magic Reishi and its tonic effects. If you could send us samples free of charge to Tokyo, our Japanese branch, we would be able to check them and take further steps. I appreciate samples of your Ganoderma Lucidum and Ganoderma Sinense.

If the samples are just what we want, we would like to place an order of 500kgs of Ganoderma Lucidum and 500kgs of Ganoderma Sinense. Please let me know your best price for the trial order.

Best regards,

David Green

Case One Analysis

Business practice

For a regular client, a concise email or phone call can fulfill the purpose of making an enquiry. In this case, however, David (the buyer) has not dealt with the seller before. It is important for him to state clearly what he wants in the enquiry. In this email, David indicated the products he intended to purchase, asked for free samples, and invited the seller to give a favorable quotation. Furthermore, he also mentioned the size of his order and market condition. This enquiry provided necessary details to enable the seller to give an appropriate offer. In other cases, the buyer may also ask for information such as catalogue, price list, specifications, minimum quantity, or even terms of payment, time of shipment and packing.

Writing strategy

This email is organized as follows:
(1) To express appreciation for the seller's interest in building business relations;
(2) To introduce his company (business scope and local market);
(3) To inform the seller of the items he is interested in, and ask the seller to send samples for his examination;
(4) To mention the possibility of placing an order and invite an offer for his desired products.

Pragmatic analysis

The buyer and the seller have not concluded any business transactions before. In replying to an email from a new business partner, it is of crucial importance for international traders to phrase their email in a friendly and polite manner. In this case, David gave a polite reply to Jenny's email for establishing business relationships. Firstly, the email began with an expression of appreciation for Jenny' previous letter (e.g. "Thanks for your interest in"). Secondly, when he asked for free samples, he used if-clauses and expressions of politeness. These pragmatic devices help to soften the tone in making his request. The example clauses in this email are "If you could send" "I appreciate" and "Please let me know".

Case Two: Offer

Dear David,

Thank you for your kind feedback.

Based on your requirements, I have applied for some free samples for you, Ganoderma Lucidum and Ganoderma Sinense, as well as our best sellers including Reishi coffee and Reishi tea. However, the delivery cost of $49 will be charged to you. Is it OK?

As is shown in our Alibaba shop, the quote for top grade organic dried Ganoderma Lucidum is $29.00 per kilogram CIF Tokyo and Ganoderma Sinense $49.00 per kilogram CIF Tokyo. However, the MOQ is 1,000 kilograms for each kind.

If you have any questions, please feel free to contact us.
Thank you.

Best regards,
Jenny

Case Two Analysis

Business practice

In replying to an enquiry, the seller should be prompt and polite, and answer all the questions mentioned in the enquiry, since an enquiry means the potential for a business cooperation. In this case, Jenny expressed her appreciation for the enquiry and willingness to provide free samples, but asked the buyer to pay for the postage. The reason is that the cost for sample delivery can be a great burden for the seller, and this move may also help her to determine whether the other party is a genuine buyer. Furthermore, she also gave quotes for several products and indicated the minimum order quantity. However, this offer did not cover all the relevant trade terms, such as payment term, delivery date, packing method, insurance, date of validity, etc. Hence, this offer only serves as a reference for the buyer and has no binding force. Jenny gave a non-firm offer possibly because the inquirer was a new client, and the size of the order he indicated did not reach the required minimum amount.

Writing strategy

This email is organized as follows:
(1) To express thanks for the enquiry;
(2) To state the availability of samples and their costs;
(3) To make a non-firm offer, indicating names of products, quality, specifications, quantity and prices;
(4) To express willingness to cooperate.

Business terms

(1) MOQ: MOQ stands for "Minimum Order Quantity" and refers to the least amount of products that a supplier is willing to sell at one time. It is set by the supplier to cover the cost of production and delivery, and ensure that they make a profit from a business deal.

(2) CIF: The acronym CIF, which stands for "cost, insurance and freight", is a trade term used to indicate whether the seller or the buyer is liable for goods that may be damaged during shipment, as well as who is responsible for paying transportation charges. This term means that the seller delivers the goods to a ship at a particular port and gets official permission for them to be exported. The seller is responsible for loading the goods on board and covering insurance costs. This term only applies to goods transported via a waterway or sea.

Case Three: Counter-offer

Dear Jenny,

Thanks for your offer. I would appreciate your samples before we negotiate on price. Please send us the samples, and I will give you feedback ASAP.

Best regards,
David

After receiving the sample, the buyer sent another email.

Dear Jenny,

We write to acknowledge the receipt of your samples with thanks and would like to place a trial order with you. However, after analyzing your quotation, we found no profit at our end. Would you like to give us a favorable price for the trial order? Another reason is that as there is no such products in our market, we need to spend a lot in marketing the efficacy of Ganoderma before it is well accepted by our customers.

Please note that our target is a total market break through and making the product a household name. Our company deals mostly with public organizations and NGOs for mass distribution; hence the samples are just a step to achieve this order and more.

Considering the huge market of Japan and Africa, could you give us a competitive CIF price?

Best regards,
David Green

Case Three Analysis

Business practice

After receiving the offer, the buyer may feel dissatisfied with the terms and conditions set out in the offer. It is common for the buyer to require alteration to the original offer. Most often a counter-offer is concerned with the price term and payment method, but the buyer may also express disagreement with various other trade terms. For instance, the buyer may seek for a lower price, ask for the reduction of minimum quantity, insist on a particular payment method, require earlier delivery, or suggest a change to packing method. In this case, David expressed his desire to place a trial order, but asked for a more favorable price. In order to make his counter-offer more persuasive, he explained that his declination of the offer was due to the little profit margin and high marketing cost. Furthermore, he described the local market environment and implied more orders in the future, so as to encourage the seller to cut the price. David did not clearly state his own price terms, but simply asked for a lower CIF price.

Writing strategy

This email is organized as follows:

(1) To acknowledge the receipt of samples with thanks, and express the intention to place an order;

(2) To make a counter proposal and ask for a more competitive quote;

(3) To give reasons for being unable to accept the offer;

(4) To explain the market condition and express the hope for a long-standing business cooperation;

(5) To reiterate the expectation for a better price.

Business terms

NGO: NGO (Non-Governmental Organization) is an organization, such as a charity, which does not make a profit, is independent of government and business, and is formed for a particular purpose for the good of the public.

Case Four: Counter-counter-offer

Dear David,

Thanks for your interest. Considering our first cooperation, I have applied for a special discount from our general manager Ms. Susan Wang and she agrees to give you a very big discount of 10% off for both products. Also, the MOQ is 1,000 kilos for each kind.

Please refer to the detailed price below:

Ganoderma Lucidum: $25.72 per kilo CIF Tokyo, and a total of $25,720 CIF Tokyo for 1,000 kilos.

Ganoderma Sinense: $44.1per kilo CIF Tokyo, and a total of $44,100 CIF Tokyo for 1,000 kilos.

N.B. This offer is open for 7 days.

As it is the first order between us, I would suggest we use L/C, rather than T/T. We do hope that this initial order will lead to many more.

Best regards,
Jenny

Case Four Analysis

Business practice

If the seller agrees with the counter-offer made by the buyer, both sides can come to an agreement and sign a contract. However, the seller may not accept the terms in the counter-offer and instead give another proposal, which constitutes a new offer. In this case, Jenny stated the trade terms more clearly, and specified the date of validity. In this re-counter offer, although Jenny agreed to lower the price by 10%, she insisted on the minimum order quantity. These decisions were made for the sake of earning a profit while starting the business. Additionally, she also clearly required the payment by L/C for the reason that it was the first cooperation between them. L/C payment may reduce the risk of the buyer's non-payment, although it involves higher banking fees.

Writing strategy

This email is organized as follows:
(1) To express thanks for the buyer's counter-offer;
(2) To make a concession in prices with a good reason (for starting the first cooperation);
(3) To provide specific terms on unit prices, method of payment and date of validity;
(4) To express the hope for further cooperation.

Business terms

(1) L/C: A letter of credit, abbreviated as L/C, is a letter from a bank guaranteeing that a buyer's payment to a seller will be received on time for the correct amount. In the event that the buyer is unable to make a payment on the purchase, the bank will be required to cover the full or remaining amount of the purchase.

(2) T/T: T/T, which stands for telegraphic transfer, is a way of remitting money overseas through any bank with Forex facility. It is just a payment method, but not payment term. So when discussing the payment term with customers, it is necessary to say "T/T+date limit", such as "T/T in advance", "T/T before shipment", "T/T within 15 days after shipment", etc..

(3) N.B.: This expression is used to make a reader pay attention to a piece of information.

Pragmatic analysis

In negotiating trade terms, business people from different cultures generally observe the Politeness Principle, otherwise, the negotiation may easily lead to communication breakdown and even the complete failure of negotiation. In this case, Jenny gave a re-counter offer, and negotiated on the price and payment terms. Firstly, she showed her courtesy by beginning the letter with a gratitude expression (e.g. "Thank you for your interest"). Secondly, in order to show her willingness to cooperate, she agreed to offer a special discount for David, which maximized benefit for him and agreed with the Tact Maxim of Politeness Principle. The example expressions are "applied for a special discount" and "give you a very big discount". Lastly, because this was the first order, she asked for L/C payment rather than advance T/T payment, which might reduce the financial risk for both sides. The utterance "I would suggest we use L/C, rather than T/T" showed that she tried to maximize the agreement between herself and the other party, as required by the Agreement Maxim of Politeness Principle. It is obvious that Jenny aimed to establish friendly relationship with the buyer and avoid communicative failures by following the Politeness Principle.

Skills Training

I. Choose the best answer.

1. We acknowledge_____thanks receipt of your letter of March 15th inquiring about the possibility of selling smart electronic appliances.

| A. with | B. in | C. for | D. to |

2. If your shirts agree_____the tastes of our market, we feel confident of placing a trial order.

| A. on | B. in | C. with | D. to |

3. We take pleasure in making you a special offer, _____our final confirmation.

| A. contributable to | B. responsible to | C. acceptable to | D. subject to |

4. We shall open an L/C_____your favor with the Standard Chartered Bank for the amount of $5,500.

| A. for | B. in | C. to | D. with |

5. From the enclosed price list you will see that we have a large_____of ladies' gloves.

| A. assort | B. assortment | C. varieties | D. collections |

6. There is a steady demand in our country_____leather gloves_____high quality.

| A. at, of | B. at, with | C. for, with | D. in, of |

7. We thank you for your letter of May 5th, _____ your purchase from us of 5,000 tons of Green Beans.

| A. confirm | B. to confirm | C. confirming | D. confirmed |

8. We are making you our quotation for shoes_____.

| A. as follows | B. as following | C. as follow | D. following |

9. Indications show that the market will advance soon. We are not_____a position to reserve the goods for you up to the end of September.

| A. for | B. in | C. at | D. with |

10. We confirm_____you a fax this morning, offering for 200 metric tons of Soybeans, subject to your reply_____us within one week.

    A. have sent, reaching   B. have sent, reached

    C. having sent, reaching   D. having sent, reached

II. Translation.

Part One

Direction: Translate the following sentences into Chinese.

1. In reply to your enquiry of June 21st, we have the pleasure of offering you Multi-floral Honey as follows.

2. Please quote us your most favorable price CIF Hamburg, stating the earliest date of shipment.

3. Should you be prepared to reduce the price by 10%, we would place a trial order with you.

4. We regret to say your prices are too high for our market, as goods from other sources are on sale here at much lower prices.

5. To acquaint you with the quality of our products, some samples have been airmailed to you under a separate cover.

Part Two

Direction: Translate the following sentences into English.

6. 如果您的订单数量超过1,000套，我们准备为您提供5%的特别折扣。

7. 我们很高兴附上我们当前的报价供您参考。
8. 贵方还盘价格与当前市场不符。
9. 该报价5天内有效，因为原材料价格正在迅速上涨。
10. 请给我方报500千克黑木耳FOB厦门的最低价。

Ⅲ. Fill in the blanks with appropriate words.

1. We have an export enquiry_____leather shoes.
2. Could you make an offer_____the items listed in your catalog?
3. The prices are subject_____our final confirmation.
4. All our prices are_____CIF basis.
5. We quote_____this article_____$10 per case FOB Guangzhou.
6. We shall place substantial order_____you, provided your new products are excellent_____quality.
7. I can give you a discount_____10%_____10,000 units.
8. _____reply_____your letter, we enclose our latest illustrated catalogue_____ _____your reference.
9. We enclose our latest catalogue and price-list_____your reference.
10. We regret we are not_____a position to satisfy your demand at present.
11. We have forwarded_____separate cover of the contract.
12. Your products can hardly sell well_____the market_____such a high price.
13. You must take_____consideration when quoting a price that we may place regular orders_____large quantities.

Ⅳ. Extensive reading.

Politeness Principle

In 1983, Geoffrey Neil Leech, a profound British linguist, published the book "Principles of Pragmatics", in which he put forword the Politeness Principle providing a model of politeness within conversation. He believed that people can use language effectively because the two parties' (speaker and hearer) observance of a series of pragmatic principles of interpersonal communication, and politeness principle is one of the important pragmatic principles. He described Politeness Principle as: all else being equal, try to weaken impolite expressions, and increase the expression of the politeness. Leech divided it into six maxims as follows:

(1) Tact Maxim is to minimize other's loss and maximize other's benefit. Tact Maxim takes the hearer or others as the starting point;

(2) Generosity Maxim is to minimize earnings of self and maximize loss of self. It requires the speaker of a conversation to reduce the self-serving information, and try to make the hearer get beneficial fit information from their discourse;

(3) Approbation Maxim is to minimize belittlement toward others and maximize praise toward others;

(4) Modesty Maxim is to minimize praise about self and maximize praise about others;

(5) Agreement Maxim is to minimize divergence with others and maintain common points with others as much as possible;

(6) Sympathy Maxim is to minimize aversion toward others and to maximize sympathy toward others as much as possible.

Leech's Politeness Principle with various maxims clearly points out the standard for differentiating polite and impolite behaviors. He indicates out that politeness principle can be combined with Grice's cooperative principle to jointly explain people's speech behavior in communication, for example, violating some maxims in cooperative principle on purpose.

Task 1. Questions:
(1) What is the Politeness Principle?
(2) What maxims do the Politeness Principle have?

Task 2. Group work
(1) What kind of maxims do the following dialogue or sentences violate? Try to use other phrases to make it more polite.
① A. Clean the dishes immediately.
   B. I hope that you will clean the dishes.
② A. I will clean the dishes
   B. Can I clean the dishes?
③ A: What do you think of my dancing today?
   B: Your dance is not bad, but I think you look a little bit chubby, and you should better lose some weight.
④ A: Your calligraphy is pretty good, and you are entitled to participate in the calligraphy competition.
   B: You are right. Everyone says that my writing has reached the level of mastery.
⑤ A: Let us go to the beach to have barbecue in this weekend, OK?
   B: What? I do not want to go, and I hate barbecue.
⑥ A: My dog is missing, and I can not find her.
   B: I hope you can not find it, and I do not want to see your dog again.

(2) Please give a response based on the following question according to the maxims of Politeness Principle.
   A: What do you think of my dancing today?

(3) If you want your colleague to help you submit a file in the office, how will you start the dialogue?

V. Writing practice.

Please have a group discussion and finish the writing task by drafting a series of negotiation emails. After you finish please do a peer review with your group members and explore what maxims of Politeness Principle have been adopted in the your emails.

Chapter 4 Order and Contract

Task Driven

Mr. David Green from South Africa Sprout International Corporation was very satisfied with the fungi products and decided to place an order with Fujian Mushroom Import & Export Co. Ltd. Both parties finally reached a deal and signed a contract. Students are divided into two groups acting as the importer and the exporter separately. One group of students writes an email to place an order while the other group drafts a Sales Confirmation according to the content of the order.

Learning Objectives

- **Knowledge objectives:** Understand contents and functions of orders and sales contracts.
- **Skill objectives:** Draft an order email; Complete a sales contract in a proper way.
- **Affective objectives**: Observe the rules and regulations of contracts.

Core Concept

4.1 Order

4.1.1 Placing an Order

An order is a request to supply a specified quantity of goods. It can be made by phone, by letter or by email after several rounds of negotiation. Usually it should include the following contents:

(1) Description of the goods, such as specification, size, quantity, quality and article number (if any);

(2) Prices (unit price as well as total price);

(3) Terms of payment;

(4) Mode of packing;

(5) Time of transportation, port of destination, and time of shipment, etc..

Sample Letter 1

Dear Sir or Madam,

Thank you for your letter of Oct. 24th sending us patterns of cotton prints. We find both quality and prices satisfactory and are pleased to give you an order for the following items with the understanding that they will be supplied from your current stock at the prices listed below:

Quantity	Pattern No.	Prices (net)
200 yards	30	25p per yard
250 yards	40	35p per yard
300 yards	50	45p per yard
		CIF London

We expect to find a good market for these cottons and hope to place further and larger orders with you in the near future.

Our usual term of payment is cash against documents and we hope it will be acceptable to you. Meanwhile should you wish to make inquiries concerning our financial standing, you may reach out to our bank:

The National Bank of London.

Please send us your confirmation of sales in duplicate.

We expect to find a good market for these cottons and hope to place further and larger orders with you in the near future.

Best regards,
John Smith

4.1.2 Confirming an Order

Confirming an order indicates the seller's acknowledgement of acceptance which is absolute and unconditional. When you accept an order, you must execute the order in accordance with the terms and conditions stipulated in it. A confirmation letter must be clear and specific about what is being confirmed or what is being changed. Meanwhile, a written purchase order should be enclosed in which all the particulars of the transaction are detailed. The following is a sample of an order sheet (Fig. 4-1).

PURCHASE ORDER

<Company Name>
<Address>
<Address>
<Contact Number>
<Default Email Address>
<Website URL>

P.O. NUMBER	DATE
23781	nn/dd/yyyy

VENDOR	CUSTOMER
NAME: <Sales Person>	NAME: John Smith
COMPANY NAME: <CompanyName>	COMPANY NAME: Redline Auto Center
ADDRESS: <Address>	ADDRESS: 16040 S. US 27, Lansing, Michigan 48906
PHONE: <Phone>	PHONE: 517-367-7010
EMAIL ADDRESS: <Email Address>	EMAIL ADDRESS: johnsmith@redline.com
SHIPPING TERMS: Freight on Board	SHIPPING METHOD: Air & Land

Code	Product Description	Quantity	Unit Price	Amount
304-98632	Brake Discs, Pads & Calipers	4	111.36	445.44
501-35587	Control Arm	2	60.93	121.86
886-19386	Suspension Lift Kit	2	399.83	799.66

Note: Payment shall be 30 days upon receipt of the items above.

Subtotal ($)		1,366.96
Discount (%)	10	136.70
Sales Tax (%)	12	164.04
Other Cost ($)		500.00
Shipping & Handling ($)		800.00
Total Amount ($)		2,694.30

Fig. 4-1 A Sample of Order Sheet
(Source: Template LAB)

Sample Letter 2

Dear Sir,

We have booked your Order No. 256 for Oolong Tea and are sending you herewith our Sales Confirmation No. BP-114 in duplicate. Please sign and return one copy to us for our file.

It is understood that a letter of credit in our favor covering the above-mentioned goods will be established immediately. We wish to point out that the stipulations in the relevant credit should strictly conform to the terms stated in our Sales Confirmation in order to avoid subsequent amendments. You may rest assured that we shall effect shipment with the least possible delay upon receipt of the credit.

We appreciate your co-operation and look forward to receiving your further orders.

Yours sincerely,

Cara Bonk

4.1.3 Declining an Order

However there are times when a seller does not intend to accept the buyer's order for some reason. Letters declining an order should be written with utmost care and an eye to good will and future business. The following explanations can be provided for declining an order:

(1) The goods required are not available;

(2) Prices and specifications have been changed;

(3) The buyers and the sellers cannot agree on some terms of the business;

(4) The buyer's credit is not in good standing;

(5) The manufacturer simply does not produce the goods ordered, etc..

Sample Letter 3

Dear Lucy,

Thank you for your order for Silk Blouse dated on July 1st.

I am sorry to tell you that due to heavy demand in the peak season, the Silk Blouse you ordered/needed is out of stock at present. Instead, we would like to recommend our new product—Cotton Blouse, which I think is more attractive in design and lower in price. If you have interests, a sample will be forwarded to you upon request.

Looking forward to your early response.

Sincerely,

John Smith

4.2 Contract

4.2.1 Defining a Contract

A contract is a formal written agreement which sets forth rights and obligations of the parties concerned. There are various types of contract, such as Sales Contract, Purchase Contract, Agency Contract, Lease Contract, and etc..

Mostly, a contract is composed of four parts: title, preamble, body and final clause/witness clause.

The preamble of a contract consists of titles, number of contract, date and place for signing the contract, parties and preface.

And the body has the following features:

(1) Descriptions of commodity: name, quality, specification, quantity, and unit price;

(2) Transportation: date of shipment, port of shipment and destination, partial shipment or transshipment permitted or not;

(3) Method of payment—L/C, collection, T/T, M/T, and D/D;
(4) Packing and shipping mark;
(5) Inspection, test/trials, acceptance;
(6) Quality guarantee;
(7) Technical training (optional);
(8) Insurance;
(9) Claim and arbitration;
(10) Validity, extension and termination.

In the end, the final clause just provides additional terms if you have, also including the validity and copies of the contract.

4.2.2 Defining a Sales Contract and Sales Confirmation

A Sales Contract is an agreement, concluded between the seller and buyer in international trade mostly from different countries, which sets forth biding obligations of the parties concerned. It is a long and comprehensive contract. By contrast, a Sales Confirmation is also a legal contract, but short and simplified. In the following, a Sales Confirmation is provided as an example.

SALES CONFIRMATION

QJ-B052

COMMODITY	:	PVC EMULSION RESIN
GRADE	:	372LD
QUANTITY	:	50 MTS
MANUFACTURER	:	VINYTHAI PUBLIC COMPANY LIMITED
COUNTRY OF ORIGIN	:	THAILAND
UNIT PRICE	:	USD 810/MT CIF XIAMEN, CHINA, L/C 60 DAYS AFTER B/L DATE
TOTAL AMOUNT	:	USD 40,500.00
PACKING	:	25KG LOOSE STUFFING IN 40FT, CONTAINER
LATEST DATE OF SHIPMENT	:	DECEMBER 2017
PORT OF LOADING	:	ANY THAILAND PORT
PORT OF DISCHARGE	:	XIAMEN, CHINA
TRANSHIPMENT	:	ALLOWED
PARTIAL SHIPMENT	:	ALLOWED
PAYMENT	:	*PAYMENT SHALL BE BY UNCONFIRMED IRREVOCABLE L/C
		*L/C SHALL NOT RESTRICT NEGOTIATION BANK
REMARKS	:	FULL SET OF B/L PRESENTED TO BANK
		THIRD PARTY DOCUMENTS ARE ACCEPTABLE
		L/C MENTION ANY BANK BY NEGOTIATION
		L/C OPEN BEFORE END OF NOV 2003 INSURANCE
		POLICY MENTION CLIAM PAYABLE IN CHINA IN
		THE SAME CURRENCY OF THE DRAFTS
ISSUING BANK MUST BE	:	BANK OF CHINA/INDUSTRIAL AND COMMERCE/
		CHINA CONSTRUCTION/ AGRICULTURE BANK OF
		CHINA/BANK OF COMMUNICATION
BUYER		SELLER/BENEFICIARY

Language Points

Words and Expressions

countersign	会签
official order	正式订单
pressing order	紧急订单
initial order	首次订单
trial order	试购订单
fresh order	新订单
repeat order	续订单
additional order	追加订单
duplicate order	重复订单
regular order	长期订单
book the order	接受订单
purchase order	订单
fulfill the order	交运订单
in duplicate	一式两份
in quadruplicate	一式四份
sales confirmation	销售确认书
sales contract	买卖合同
donation contract	赠与合同
loan contract	借款合同
leasing contract	租赁合同
work-for-hire contract	承揽合同
carriage contract	运输合同
technology contract	技术合同
safe-keeping contract	保管合同
warehousing contract	仓储合同
brokerage contract	居间合同
agency agreement	委托代理协议
partnership agreement	合伙协议
confidentiality agreement	保密协议
non-compete agreement	竞业禁止协议
contract for supply of power, water, gas or heat	供用电、水、气、热力合同
financial leasing contract	融资租赁合同
construction project contract	建设工程合同
agency appointment contract	委托合同
commission agency contract	行纪合同

shares assignment agreement 股份转让协议
employment agreement 聘用协议

Sentences

1. We expect to find a good market for the above product and hope to place further and larger orders with you in the near future.

我方期待着为以上产品开辟一个良好的市场,并希望在将来向贵方下更多更大的订单。

2. We have pleasure in sending you an order for cosmetics.

兹寄去化妆品订单一份。

3. This is a trial order. Please send us 50 sets only so that we may tap the market. If successful, we will give you large orders in the future.

这是一份试订单。我们试订50台以开发市场。如果成功,随后必将大量订购。

4. Please repeat last season's order for 400 sets of textbooks.

请按上季订单,再订购教材400套。

5. We are willing to purchase 50 cases of china tea sets, provided that you sell them at a price not exceeding 100.00 RMB per set.

我们欲购买50箱陶瓷茶具,前提是单价不超过人民币100元。

6. Please supply in assorted colors: preferably 6 dozens each of red, yellow, green, blue and brown.

请按下列颜色搭配供货,最好红、黄、绿、蓝及棕色各6打。

7. We want the goods to be exactly the same quality as those you previously supplied us.

我们希望此批订货质量与上批供应的完全一样。

8. With reference to your quotation, we enclose our order for immediate delivery.

提及你方报价,我们随附订单,要求立即装运。

9. The maximum we can supply is only half of your order because our stock is low at present.

由于目前存货不多,最大供货量仅为你方订货量的一半。

10. Although your price is below our level, we accept this order as an exception in order to initiate business with you.

尽管你方价格偏低,但考虑到这是初笔交易,我们破例接受这一订单。

11. We are compelled to decline this order because the price you asked for is out of line with the ruling market.

由于你方要价与现行市价不符,所以我们只好谢绝你方订单。

12. We are pleased to inform you that we have booked the order placed by you yesterday.

很高兴的告诉您昨日你们下的订单已经确认。

13. We hope our products will satisfy your needs and hope to serve you again.

希望我方产品使你们满意,今后再来惠顾。

14. We can not accept any fresh orders because we are fully committed. But as soon as fresh supplies come in, we shall contact you without delay.

由于订单太多,我们不能接受新订单,但一旦有新货,我们将立即与你方联系。

15. We can offer you a substitute which is the same price and similar quality as the goods ordered.

我们可以提供给你方价格一致、质量基本相同的替代品。

16. It is regrettable to see that the chemical content of Item 073 is not up to the percentage contracted.

很遗憾，073号商品所含化学成分没达到合同规定的百分比。

17. Please note that the 2,000 sets of computers under Contract No.0426 have been ready for some time, but your covering L/C has not reached us yet. Please open the L/C as soon as possible so that we may arrange the shipment.

请注意，第0426合约下的2000台计算机备妥待运已久，但至今未收到你方的信用证。望速将其开来，以便安排装运。

18. We hereby certify to the best of our knowledge that the foregoing statement is true and correct and all available information and data have been supplied herein, and that we agree to provide documentary proof upon your request.

兹证明上述声明内容真实、正确无误，并提供了全部现有的资料数据。应贵方要求，我们同意出具证明文件。

19. This Contract is hereby made and concluded by and between ABC Co. (hereinafter referred to as Party A) and CAR Co. (hereinafter referred to as Party B) on June 6th, 2018, in Shanghai, China, on the principle of equality and mutual benefit and through amicable consultation.

本合同双方，ABC公司（以下称甲方）与CAR公司（以下称乙方），在平等互利基础上，通过友好协商，于2018年6月6日在中国上海，特签订本合同。

20. If the quantity of the goods does not conform to that stipulated in the contract, the importer will reject the goods.

如果货物数量不符合合同规定，进口商将拒收货物。

21. If you agree to the above conditions, we will call it a deal and prepare the sales contract.

如果你同意上述条件，我们就成交并准备销售合同。

22. As it is specifically stipulated in the contract, the relevant L/C should reach the seller 15 days before the month of shipment, that is, the L/C covering the goods to be shipped in May should reach us no later than April 15th.

正如合同中具体规定，有关信用证必须在装货月前15天到达卖方，也就是说，5月装运的货物的信用证必须不迟于4月15日到达我方手中。

23. As stipulated in the contract, we have airmailed you a set of copies of shipping documents upon the completion of shipment.

按照合同规定，我方已在货物装船后立即航寄你方一套装船单据的副本。

24. The Seller shall not be held responsible for failure or delay in delivery of the entire lot or a portion of the goods under this Sales Confirmation in consequence of any Force Majeure incidents.

本确认书内所述全部或部分商品，如因人力不可抗拒的原因，以至不能履约或延迟交货，售方概不负责。

25. This contract will come into effect as soon as it is signed by two parties.
本合同一经双方签订，立即生效。

Case One: An order from the importer

Hi Jenny,

Thanks for your kind help. As you have helped me cut the price, I would like to place a bigger order to meet your MOQ. Attached is the PO.

Ganoderma Lucidum: $25.72 per kilo CIF Tokyo, and a total of $25,720 CIF Tokyo for 1,000 kilos.

Ganoderma Sinense: $44.1per kilo CIF Tokyo, and a total of $44,100 CIF Tokyo for 1,000 kilos.

Could you please help us with the PI? We will do L/C.

Kind regards,

David

Case One Analysis

Business practice

In placing an order, many companies prefer to use order forms, rather than spell out all the terms in an email. In this case, David sent an order and attached a copy of purchase order form, which helped to clearly state the terms of transaction and avoid missing essential details. It is crucial for David to ensure the accuracy of all the details before sending out the order, since an order form often provides the basis for preparing the contract draft and establishing a letter of credit. Even a minor mistake in the purchase order form may lead to unexpected troubles or even the complete failure of a business deal.

Writing strategy

This email is organized as follows:

(1) To state the intention to place an order by referring to the previous correspondence;

(2) To give a detailed description of the goods ordered including names of commodity, quantity, unit prices, etc. (as shown in the purchase order);

(3) To request the seller to send a proforma invoice.

Generally, an order form includes the information as below:

(1) the name of commodities ordered;

(2) the description of commodities (such as size, weight, color, material);

(3) the quantity ordered;

(4) unit price;

(5) total amount;

(6) method of payment;

(7) date of delivery;

(8) method of delivery;

(9) authorized signature;

(10) other relevant information, including the order number, validity of the order, port of loading, port of destination, etc.

Business terms

(1) PO: Purchase order (abbreviated as PO) is a formal document requesting the supply of goods or services, giving details of the goods, price, conditions of delivery and payment, etc.

(2) PI: A proforma invoice, abbreviated as PI, is a preliminary bill of sale sent to buyers in advance of a shipment or delivery of goods. The invoice will typically describe the purchased items and other important information, such as the shipping weight and transportation charges.

Case Two: A contract from the exporter

Dear David,

Thanks for your PO. Attached is the contract. Once it is signed, I will do the PO and arrange for shipment.

Kind regards,

Enclosure: Sales Contract.

Sales Contract

Contract No.: CEFPE10298665

Date: March 2nd, 2022

Seller: Fujian Mushroom Import & Export Co., Ltd., China

Buyer: South Africa Sprout International Corporation, Japan Branch

This Sales Contract is made by and between the Seller and the Buyer whereby the Seller agrees to sell and the Buyer agrees to buy the under-mentioned goods according to the terms and conditions stipulated below:

Commodity	N.W.	Quantity	U/Price	Amount
Ganoderma Lucidum	1,000KGS	1,000KGS	$25.72 per kilo CIF Tokyo	$25,720 CIF Tokyo
Ganoderma Sinense	1,000KGS	1,000KGS	$44.1 per kilo CIF Tokyo	$44,100 CIF Tokyo
Total	2,000KGS	2,000KGS		$69,850

(1) The Seller is allowed to load 5% more or less and the price shall be calculated according to the unit price.

(2) Shipping Marks: SASIC TOKYO No. 1～1000.

(3) Insurance: To be covered by the Seller for 110% of the invoice value against All Risks and War Risk as per the relevant Ocean Marine Cargo Clauses of the People's Insurance Company of China. If other coverage or an additional insurance amount is required, the Buyer must have the consent of the Seller before shipment, and the additional premium is to be borne by the Buyer.

(4) Port of Shipment: Fuzhou, China.

(5) Port of Destination: Tokyo, Japan.

(6) Time of Shipment: During April 2022, allowing partial shipments and transshipment.

(7) Terms of Payment: The Buyer shall open with a bank acceptable to the Seller an Irrevocable Letter of Credit at sight to reach the Seller 30 days before the time of shipment specified, valid for negotiation in China until the 15th day after the aforesaid time of shipment. The Buyer shall establish the covering Letter of Credit before March 1st 2022, failing which the Seller reserves the right to rescind the contract without further notice.

(8) Commodity Inspection: It is mutually agreed that the Certificate of Quality and Weight issued by the State General Administration for Quality Supervision and Inspection and Quarantine of P. R. China at the port of shipment shall be taken as the basis of delivery.

(9) Discrepancy and Claim: Any claim by the Buyer on the goods shipped shall be filed within 30 days after the arrival of the goods at the port of destination and supported by a survey report issued by a surveyor approved by the Seller. Claims with respect to matters within the responsibility of the insurance company or of the shipping company will not be considered or entertained by the Seller.

(10) Force Majeure: If shipment of the contracted goods is prevented or delayed in whole or in part due to Force Majeure, the Seller shall not be liable for non-shipment or late shipment of the goods under this Contract. However, the Seller shall notify the Buyer by fax or e-mail and furnish the latter within 15 days by registered airmail with a certificate issued by the China Council for the Promotion of International Trade attesting such event or events.

(11) Arbitration: All disputes arising out of the performance of or relating to this Contract shall be settled amicably through negotiation. In case no settlement can be reached through negotiation, the case shall then be submitted to the Foreign Economic and Trade Arbitration Commission of the China Council for the Promotion of International Trade, Beijing, China, for arbitration in accordance with its Rules of Procedure. The award of the arbitration is final and binding upon both parties.

(12) Governing Law: This Contract shall be governed by the United Nations Convention on Contracts for the International Sale of Goods.

(13) Other Terms: This contract shall be made out in original and duplicate, one for each party and shall be binding on both parties.

THE SELLER (Signature)   THE BUYER (Signature)

Case Two Analysis

Business practice

After receiving the order, Jenny wrote to accept the order and attached a formal contract, confirming the agreed terms. A well-drafted contract clearly defines the rights and obligations of both parties and reduces the risk of possible trade disputes. Sometimes, the buyer or seller may ask the other party to countersign the purchase order or sales contract for their records. To show her acceptance of the order, Jenny also mentioned that she would prepare Proforma Invoice and arranged for the execution of order. However, under special circumstances, the seller may also decline the buyer's order. The reasons are that the seller cannot supply the goods from stock, or cannot accept the terms set out in the order.

Writing strategy

This email is organized as follows:

(1) To express thanks for the order;

(2) To mention the attached sales contract, in which the rights and responsibilities of both the buyer and the seller are spelled out;

(3) To inform the buyer of her immediate action (to do the PI and arrange cargo shipment).

Generally, a sales contract includes the following parts, subject to minor changes:

(1) Beginning part: the name of the seller and buyer, contract number, and the date and place for signing the contract;

(2) Main body: specific terms of the contract (rights and obligations of both parties), such as commodity, specification, quantity, price, payment, packing, delivery and insurance. Some contracts also contain clauses such as inspection, claim for loss, arbitration and force majeure, etc.;

(3) Ending part: the number of copies, signature of both parties, applicable law and practice, etc..

I. Choose the best answer.

1. Following your order_____400 pieces of electronic toys last year, we are pleased to receive your order No.456_____the same quantity.

  A. with, for   B. of, of   C. of, for   D. for, of

2. We_____your terms satisfactory and now send you our order for 2 sets of the generator.

  A. find   B. believe   C. think   D. trust

3. We place an order provided your goods can be supplied_____stock.

  A. out   B. out of   C. from   D. in

4. The goods are urgently needed. We_____hope you will deliver them at once.
   A. therefore   B. so   C. that   D. should
5. We place this order_____the understanding that the discount is 10%.
   A. in   B. for   C. on   D. through
6. In this case, the buyer_____cancel the contract.
   A. could
   B. may have to
   C. has the right to
   D. reserve the right to
7. As agreed upon in our negotiations, payment_____L/C.
   A. by   B. is to be made by   C. will   D. is by
8. We regret to report that a consignment of silk piece goods_____Order No.567 has not been delivered.
   A. with   B. in   C. on   D. under
9. We feel sorry to say that the rugs supplied_____Order No.456 have not yet reached us.
   A. by   B. for   C. with   D. to
10. _____ the present market trend, we have to say that our price is really the best we can quote.
   A. With   B. On   C. Because   D. For

Ⅱ. Translation.

Part One

Direction: Translate the following sentences into Chinese.

1. We are pleased to receive your Order No. 6821 covering three metric tons of Green Tea Extract and 5,000 Porcelain Tea Sets.

2. It is our regret that we cannot at present entertain any fresh orders because of our heavy commitments.

3. Your samples received favourable reaction from our customers, and we are pleased to place our order for 500 cartons.

4. As the prices quoted are exceptionally low and likely to rise, we would advise you to place your order without delay.

5. We are sending you our Sales Confirmation No.YH1066 in duplicate, one copy of which is to be countersigned and returned for our record.

Part Two

Direction: Translate the following sentences into English.

6. 如果质量达到我们的期望，我们将在不久后续签订单。
7. 由于最近花生的大量需求，我们无法承诺在下个月前交付任何新订单。
8. 很遗憾，我们无法以两个月前的报价履行订单。
9. 如果您在6月10日之前下订单，我们可以向您保证及时发货。
10. 我方确认以你方第652号订单中规定的价格供应6吨核桃仁，并将尽快安排发货。

III. Fill in the contract form in English with the particulars given in the following letter.

敬启者：

很高兴从您 8 月 1 日来信中得知您已接受我方 7 月 5 日的报盘。作为答复，我方确认向贵公司出售 200 个 200 毫升茶杯，200 个 500 毫升的茶壶，CIF 价分别为 10 美元和 15 美元。以上产品将都用纸箱包装，1 个纸箱可容纳 40 个茶杯或 10 个茶壶。由卖方按发票金额 110%投保一切险及战争险，预计 2015 年 9 月从中国上海运往香港，唛头由我方决定，以不可撤销的、保兑的即期信用证付款，信用证必须在装运前 3 天到达我方。按照惯例，信用证议付有效期为最后装运期后第 15 天在中国到期。

兹随函将我方 8 月 5 日在北京所签第 291 号确认书一式两份寄与你方，望查收。请会签并返回我方一份。

此致

敬礼！

上海横大国际贸易有限公司
经理：XXX 谨上

Sales Confirmation

No. 291

Sellers: __(1)__
Buyers: Fields Inc

This Contract is made by and between the Buyer and Seller, whereby the Buyer agrees to buy and the Seller agrees to sell the under-mentioned commodity according to the terms and conditions stipulated below:

Commodity: (2)_____
Quantity: (3)_____
Unit Price: (4)_____
Total Value: (5)_____
Packing: (6)_____
Insurance: (7)_____
Time of Shipment: (8)_____
Port of Shipment: Shanghai
Port of Destination: (9)_____
Shipping Marks: at Sellers' option
Terms of Payment: (10)_____

IV. Extensive reading.

As early as the 1950s, Goffman (E. Goffman) put forward the "Face Theory" aiming at the phenomenon of saving the counterpart's face emerging in speech communication. He thinks that all the people would involve the face problem during any communication process, which is one of the rules of human behavior and exists in all kinds of human activities. Human behavior is constrained by their faces, meanwhile, people also expect the other side in their communication to save their faces. That is to say, the best method for one person to save self-face is to maintain other's faces. Therefore, people should save the face of the other side in interpersonal communications, thereby avoiding embarrassment and maintaining good relationship of both sides.

All rational social members have two kinds of faces: positive face and negative face. Positive face means that one hopes to be praised for his own behavior and manners; while negative face means that one hope his own freedom is not infringed by others. Besides, polite behavior is also divided into two types during processes of people's speech communication: positive politeness and negative politeness. The former type refers to the positive requirements for maintaining the other side's face.

Task:
1. What are positive face and negative face?
2. How does the face affect people's behavior?
3. What is saving face and losing face in Chinese culture?
4. How do you think Chinese face affects people's communication behaviors?

V. Writing practice.

Please finish the writing tasks including an order email and a Sales Confirmation. Afterwards, you can have a peer review for assessing the result.

Chapter 5 Payment and Documentation

Task Driven

South Africa Sprout International Corporation opened a Letter of Credit (L/C) as requested by the seller and had the advising bank notify the seller in a timely manner. However, Fujian Mushroom Import & Export Co. Ltd. found 3 discrepancies between the L/C and the contract. Please work in groups to write an email of L/C amendment on behalf of the seller (Fujian Mushroom Import & Export Co. Ltd.).

Learning Objectives

• **Knowledge objectives:** Tell the difference among remittance, collection, and L/C; Understand the functions of draft.
• **Skill objectives:** Draft an amendment email; Fill in various documents under the L/C; Know how to make an examination and amendment of L/C.
• **Affective objectives:** Realize the importance of L/C in international trade.

Core Concept

5.1 Terms of Payment

Terms of payment refer to a series of activities or operations facilitating the movement of funds from one destination to the other. They are classified into remittance, collection and L/C.

5.1.1 Remittance

Remittance is one of banking customer services, in which funds are transferred from buyers to sellers. Remittance includes Mail Transfer (M/T), Telegraphic Transfer (T/T) and Demand Draft (D/D). M/T means that the remitting bank sends the remittance instruction by mail while T/T indicates that the instruction is sent by telecommunication system. By contrast, D/D states that the remittance instruction can be sent to the paying bank by demand draft which is drawn by the remitting bank on the paying bank in favor of the exporter. Therefore, M/T has a lower charge but is very slow while T/T is faster but more expensive. D/D may have the lowest charges but can be transferred to the third party. In a word, remittance is often used in cash with order, payment in advance and open account business.

5.1.2 Collection

Collection is an arrangement whereby the seller draws a draft on the buyer and authorizes its bank to collect. In the course of collection, banks only provide the service of collecting the documents from the seller and remitting the money to them. However, if the buyer doesn't make payment in advance, the bank will not pay the seller.

Documentary collection can be classified into Documents against Payment (D/P) and Documents against Acceptance (D/A). D/P indicates that the collecting bank releases the documents to the importer only upon full and immediate cash payment. So we have D/P at sight and D/P after sight. The former means that the importer presents the sight draft while the latter means the importer presents the time draft.

By contrast, D/A indicates that the collecting bank will release the documents against the draft accepted by the importer. Therefore the importer will get the documents and then make payment when the draft is at maturity.

5.1.3 Letter of Credit (L/C)

5.1.3.1 Definition

A L/C is the written promise of a bank that acts at the request and on the instruction of the applicant and undertakes to pay the beneficiary the amount specified in the credit, provided that the terms and conditions of the credit are observed by the beneficiary.

5.1.3.2 Characteristics

The L/C has the following three characteristics:
(1) Banker's credit. The issuing bank undertakes to effect payment, provided the documents are in compliance with the terms and conditions of L/C;
(2) A self-sufficient instrument. Although the credit is issued on the basis of the sales

contract, banks are not bound by such contract;

(3) Dealing with documents. The bank only deals with documents under the L/C, not with goods which the documents may be related to.

5.1.3.3 Classification

There are various types of L/C as follows:

(1) Revocable and irrevocable L/C. An irrevocable letter of credit cannot be modified, amended or withdrawn by either the opening bank or the buyer before the expiry date of credit without the agreement of the beneficiary; a revocable letter of credit can be canceled or amended at any moment within the credit validity without notice to the beneficiary;

(2) Documentary and clean L/C. Documentary L/C should call for some documents in accordance with the terms of the credit while clean L/C does not require any shipping documents during the process of payment;

(3) Sight and usance L/C. Under a sight L/C, the negotiating bank makes payment immediately upon the presentation of the sight draft and shipping documents as stipulated in L/C by the seller. Under a usance L/C, the negotiating bank does not make payment immediately. The negotiating bank hands over the draft and documents to the opening bank. The opening bank does not pay the money immediately either, who just accepts the draft and makes payment when the time draft falls due.

A sample of L/C can be found in Appendix One.

5.2 Documentation

Documentation plays an important part in international trade. It refers to the preparation and examination of documents involved in an international transaction. The major purpose is to provide a detailed and complete description of the goods so as to be processed correctly for shipment, packing, insurance, payment, customs clearance, etc. With the proper documents, the exporters will be able to send the goods out of the countries and collect payment, while the importers can take delivery of the goods at the destination.

There are several broad categories of documents in international trade including commercial documents, financial documents, insurance documents, shipping documents, etc. They are closely related to payment terms, such as L/C.

Commercial documents.

(1) Commercial invoice;

(2) Packing/Weight/Measurement list.

Financial documents.

(1) Draft;

(2) Promissory note;

(3) Check.

Shipping documents.
(1) Ocean/Airway B/L;
(2) Shipping advice.

Insurance documents.
(1) Insurance policy;
(2) Insurance certificate.

Other documents.
(1) Certificate of Origin;
(2) Beneficiary's Certificate.

Please refer to Appendix Two for the samples of documents.

Language points

Words and Expressions

Mail Transfer	信汇
Telegraphic Transfer	电汇
Demand Transfer	票汇
D/P at sight	即期付款交单
D/P after sight	远期付款交单
D/A	承兑交单
irrevocable L/C	不可撤销信用证
documentary L/C	跟单信用证
sight L/C	即期信用证
usance L/C	远期信用证
clean L/C	光票信用证
confirmed L/C	保兑信用证
opening/issuing bank	开证行
transferrable L/C	可转让信用证
advising/notifying bank	通知银行
negotiating bank	议付行
beneficiary	受益人
drawer	开票人
drawee bank	受票银行
cash with order	订货付款
payment in advance	预付
open account	记账交易
sight/demand bill	即期汇票
time/usance bill	远期汇票

presentation	提示，提交
acceptance	承兑
blank endorsement	空白背书
dishonor	拒付
recourse	追索
promissory note	本票
amendment	改证
commission	佣金
settlement	结算
tenor	票期
days of grace	宽限期
discrepancy	不符（点）
expiry date	失效日期
formality	手续
at a fixed date	定日付款
honor the draft	付款
pay at 30 days after sight	见票后 30 天付款
pay at 30 days after date of draft	出票后 30 天付款
pay at 30 days date of B/L	出提单 30 日后付款
Letter of Credit available by/against draft at sight	即期信用证
L/C available by draft at 30 days after sight	远期 30 天信用证

Sentences

1. The shipment under your Credit No.F11 has been ready for quite some time, but up to the present we have not received any news of L/C.

你方 F11 号信用证下的货物已备妥有一段时间了，但直到现在为止，我们仍未收到关于信用证的任何消息。

2. We regret that we could not ship the goods by May only because of the delay of your L/C.

很遗憾，由于你方信用证迟开，我们无法在 5 月装运货物。

3. Referring to our Contract No.361, we have not received any information from you about your letter of credit which should have reached us before July 15th, 2018.

关于你方 361 号合同，我们没有收到任何信用证的相关消息，而信用证本应在 2018 年 7 月 15 日前到达我处的。

4. In spite of our repeated requests, still we have not received your letter of credit up to now. Please open the credit by cable immediately, otherwise, we cannot effect shipment in January.

尽管再三催请开证，我方仍未收到信用证，请立即电开，否则无法在 1 月交货。

5. According to the stipulations in our Sales Confirmation No.123, you should send us your L/C one month before the date of shipment.

根据 123 销售合同规定，你们应在发货前 1 个月把信用证寄给我们。

6. Please amend L/C No. 333 to " This L/C will expire on 12th March , 2018 in China."

请把第 333 号信用证改为："该信用证将于 2018 年 3 月 12 日在中国到期"。

7. We have received your relevant L/C, but to our regret it contains the following discrepancies.

已收到你方有关信用证，但很遗憾，内容有如下不符。

8. Please advise your bankers to make the necessary amendment.

请通知你方银行做必要的改证。

9. Please insert the word "about" before the quantity of the goods in your L/C No. 11.

请把单词"about"插入到第 11 号信用证中商品数量之前。

10. Please delete the clause "Partial shipment and transshipment allowed".

请把"允许分批装船和转船"这一条款删除。

11. Please amend L/C No.99 as follows:

A. Amount to be increased up to US$ 25,000.

B. Validity to be extended to 15th December.

请将 99 号信用证做如下修改：

A. 金额提高到 25,000 美元。

B. 有效期延至 12 月 15 日。

12. On examination, we find that the amount of your L/C is insufficient. Please increase the unit price US$ 20 to US$ 30, and total amount to US$ 4,500.

经审核发现，你方信用证金额不足。请把单价从 20 美元提高到 30 美元，总金额达到 4500 美元。

13. Please extend the shipment date and validity of your L/C to June 30th and July 15th respectively and make sure that the amendment advice reaches us by August 1st.

请把装运期和信用证有效期分别延长至 6 月 30 日和 7 月 15 日，并确保信用证修改通知在 8 月 1 日之前到达我处。

14. The amendment advice should reach us by April 15th, failing which you must extend the validity of the L/C to the end of this year.

改证通知应在 4 月 15 日之前送达，否则你们只能把信用证有效期延长到今年年底。

15. The shipment covered by your Credit No. 432 has been ready for quite some time, but the amendment advice has not yet arrived, and now an extension of 15 days is required.

依据第 432 号信用证，货物已备妥一段时间。但是改证通知至今未收到，因此现在只能申请 15 天延期了。

16. I have given you our amendment instruction for a week. Please instruct the bank to make an amendment as soon as possible.

改证说明已发送一周，请通知贵方银行尽快修改信用证。

17. Please note that payment should be made by confirmed and irrevocable L/C available by draft at sight, allowing partial shipment and transshipment.

请注意，付款时以保兑、不可撤销、允许分装和转船、见票即付的信用证付款。

18. Our terms of payment are by irrevocable documentary L/C in our favor, payable by 30 days' draft reaching us one month ahead of shipment.

我们的付款方式是以不可撤销的跟单信用证支付，见远期 30 天汇票付款，信用证需在装运前一个月到达我方。

19. We regret that we can not accept D/P after the goods arrive at the port of destination.

很抱歉我方不能接受货到目的港后凭单付款的支付方式。

20. In view of the long standing friendly relations, we exceptionally accept D/P at 60 days sight.

鉴于双方长期友好关系，此次我们破例接受 D/P 60 天付款。

21. Provided such drafts are drawn and presented in accordance with the terms of this credit, we hereby engage with the drawers, endorsers and bona-fide holders that the said drafts shall be honored on presentation.

凡根据本信用证的条件开出并提示的汇票，本行保证对出票背书人及善意持有人履行付款义务。

22. Draft(s) drawn under this credit must be negotiated in China on or before May 1st, after which this credit expires.

此信用证的汇票必须在 5 月 1 日或之前在中国议付，此日之后汇票满期。

23. Full set of clean on board ocean Bills of Lading in 3 originals, made out to order and blank endorsed.

全套清洁、已装船海运提单（3 份原件），开出凭指示，空白背书。

24. "Shipping on Board" Bills of Lading are essential and the statements "Freight paid" must appear thereon. Bills of Lading must cover shipment as detailed below. Short form Bills of Lading are not acceptable.

"已装船"提单应作为基本条件，并在其上注明"运费已付"的字样。提单必须包括下列详述的货物。简式提单恕不接受。

25. Special conditions: Documents have to be presented within 14 days after the date of issue of bills of lading or other shipping documents.

特别条款：单据必须在提单或其他装船单据签发日期之后 14 天内提示。

Case One: Urging the Establishment of L/C

Dear David,

Referring to our Sales Contract No.CEFPE 10298665 dated March 2nd, 2022, we regret to say that your L/C has not yet reached us up to the time of writing. This has caused us much inconvenience as we have already made preparations for shipment according to the stipulations of the said S/C.

You must be aware that the terms and conditions of the contract once signed should be strictly observed, and failure to abide by them will mean violation of the contract. If you refer to our sales contract, you will see the clause reading:

"The Buyer shall establish the covering Letter of Credit before March 1st, 2022, failing which the Seller reserves the right to rescind the contract without further notice."

The goods you ordered have been ready for quite some time and the demand for the goods has been so great that we find it hard to keep them for any longer. However, considering our friendly business relations, we are prepared to wait for your L/C, which must reach us no later than March 15th, 2022.

Your cooperation in this respect would be appreciated.

Best regards,
Jenny

Case One Analysis

Business practice

It is a common practice for the buyer to open a letter of credit reaching the seller at least 15 days before delivery, which allows the seller to arrange shipment. In this case, the buyer failed to open the L/C within the time limit indicated in the sales contract. Hence, Jenny wrote to express regret of not having received the L/C and reminded the importer of expediting the establishment of the covering L/C. This email was strongly worded, and Jenny even hinted at the possibility of canceling the contract. However, it is usually recommended that the first letter urging the buyer to open the L/C should be a polite reminder, rather than a direct criticism of the buyer. After all, the aim of this kind of correspondence is to persuade the buyer to cooperate rather than to offend him. The reason why Jenny gave a strong remark might be that it was the seller's market and the goods were ready for shipment.

Writing strategy

This email is organized as follows:

(1) To refer to the relevant sales contract;

(2) To emphasize the fact of not having received the relevant L/C;

(3) To remind the buyer of the consequence of the failure to establish L/C;

(4) To urge the buyer to expedite L/C establishment and set a deadline;

(5) To express the seller's expectations.

Case Two: Amendment of L/C

Dear David,

We are glad to receive your L/C No. MOS-D02 under the S/C No. CEFPE 10298665.

We have carefully observed the terms and conditions stipulated in your L/C, but we regret to inform you that we found some discrepancies in the L/C which you have to instruct your bank to make the following amendments:

(1) The expiry place of the L/C should be "in China", instead of "at our counter";

(2) The total amount should be "USD69,850.00, in words Sixty-nine Thousand Eight Hundred Fifty only", instead of "USD59,850.00, in words as Fifty-nine Thousand Eight Hundred Fifty only";

(3) The shipment is made from "Fuzhou" to Tokyo, not from "Fuzou";

(4) The insurance should be covered for the 110% of the full invoice value, instead of "130%";

(5) Please delete the clause "shipment per pacific international line".

We hope the amendment to the L/C can reach here before March 20th, 2022, or the shipment can not be effected as requested. Your immediate response is being expected.

Best regards,
Jenny

Case Two Analysis

Business practice

In this case, Jenny examined the stipulations in the L/C, but found some discrepancies between the L/C and sales contract. To avoid the risk of the bank refusing to pay, Jenny sent an email to the buyer, requesting him to make amendments to a few clauses in L/C. Furthermore, she reminded the buyer that the late arrival of L/C might lead to the postponement of delivery.

In the amendment of L/C, some useful expressions particularly for the amendment should be adopted so as to indicate how to amend the clause. Some examples are shown as follows:

(1) find some discrepancy　　　　　　　　发现不符点
(2) instruct the bank to make an amendment　　通知银行改证
(3) …instead of　　　　　　　　　　　…应该是…条款而不是…条款
(4) in words　　　　　　　　　　　　大写是
(5) The quantity should be increased from… to …　数量从…增加至…
(6) Please delete…　　　　　　　　　请删除
(7) amend…(so as) to read　　　　　　将…改为
(8) amend…as　　　　　　　　　　　将…改为
(9) rather than　　　　　　　　　　　而非，而不是
(10) cross off　　　　　　　　　　　　删除
(11) insert/add/ incorporate　　　　　　插入
(12) in conformity with/ in line with　　与…相符

Writing strategy

This email is organized as follows:

(1) To express happiness to receive the L/C under the sales contract;
(2) To give a reason for amending the clauses in the L/C;
(3) To explain how to amend the L/C;
(4) To express hope for an early reply with the renewed L/C.

The information in a typical L/C is as follows:

(1) The number of L/C;
(2) The type of the credit;
(3) The contract number;
(4) The relevant participants, such as the applicant, opening bank, beneficiary, advising bank, etc;
(5) The amount of the credit;

(6) The date and place of the credit expiry;

(7) The description of the commodities, including name of commodity, quantity, specifications, unit price, packing, etc;

(8) The port of shipment, the port of destination, the time of shipment, and whether partial shipment or transshipment is allowed;

(9) Documents required;

(10) The period of presentation;

(11) Charges;

(12) Instructions to the negotiating bank;

(13) The signature of the opening bank;

(14) The uniform customs and practice for documentary credits.

Case Three: Extension of L/C

Dear David,

As stipulated in S/C No. CEFPE10298665, shipment could be made in April provided your L/C reached us no later than March 20th. However, we received your L/C only yesterday and it is absolutely impossible for us to ship the goods by the end of April.

In this circumstance, we regret to ask you to extend the above L/C to April 6th and May 1st for shipment and negotiation respectively, with the amendment to reach us by the 30th of March. Otherwise shipment will be further postponed.

We look forward to receiving the relevant amendment at an early date and thank you in advance.

Best regards,
Jenny

Case Three Analysis

Business practice

In the L/C, there are stipulations on the latest date of shipment, the period for presentation and the date of expiry. There should be around two weeks apart between the date of shipment and the date of expiry, so that the seller can have enough time to prepare for the presentation of documents. In this case, Jenny made her request to extend L/C and postpone the delivery because of the buyer's failure in establishing the L/C in accordance with the stipulations in the sales contract.

Writing strategy

(1) To acknowledge the receipt of the L/C;

(2) To explain the reason for L/C extension;

(3) To make an request to extend the negotiation date of L/C and date of shipment;

(4) To express expectations for receiving the new L/C.

I. Choose the best answer.

1. Seldom_____accepted payment by D/P.
   A. we have   B. have we   C. we have not   D. have we not

2. We must point out that_____your L/C reaches us before the end of this month, we shall not be able to effect shipment within the stipulated time limit.
   A. if   B. unless   C. in case   D. in case of

3. _____, the buyers have urged us to expedite shipment of their order.
   A. The season approaching
   B. The season is approaching
   C. As the season is approaching
   D. The season was approaching

4. We believe we can_____if you agree with the payment by D/P at sight.
   A. end a business
   B. materialize the business
   C. result the business
   D. put the business through

5. In accordance with our agreement, we have_____at 30 days' sight for the amount of the enclosed invoice.
   A. drawn on you   B. written to you   C. called on you   D. advised you

6. You can_____a draft at 30 days' sight through Bank of China for the full CIF value of the invoice.
   A. establish for us   B. issue to us   C. open against us   D. draw on us

7. The Bank of Japan, Tokyo, will soon_____a credit in your favor to be available until September 30 next.
   All of the following words can suitably complete the sentence EXCEPT:
   A. draw   B. issue   C. establish   D. open

8. Concerning the_____L/C, we wish to inform you that several clauses need to be amended.
   A. caption   B. title   C. captioned   D. subjected

9. When we received the documents, they were_____.
   A. blank endorsed
   B. endorsed in blank
   C. blankly endorsed
   D. endorsed blankly

10. Since your request for the alteration of destination came at such short_____, we have to ask you to extend the shipment and validity of the L/C.
    A. notation   B. note   C. notice   D. notification

II. Translation.

Part One

Direction: Translate the following sentences into Chinese.

1. Please delete from the L/C the clause "All bank charges are for beneficiary's account".

2. Payment is to be made by sight draft drawn under an irrevocable and confirmed letter of credit without recourse for the full amount.

3. The L/C should be established in strict accordance with the stipulations of the contract so as to avoid unnecessary amendments.

4. Please insert the word "approximately" before the quantity and amount in your L/C as it is impossible for us to ship the goods in the exact quantity as contracted.

5. With reference to the goods under your P/O No. KRIT210518, we wish to draw your attention to the fact that we have not received your payment of 30% of the total value by T/T.

Part Two
Direction: Translate the following sentences into English.
6. 鉴于我们双方长期的友好关系，此次我们破例接受 D/P 60 天付款。
7. 付款方式为电汇，即随定单预付 30%定金，传真提单副本后支付 70%余款给我们。
8. 请修改相关信用证以允许货物部分装运。
9. 请尽最大努力加快开立信用证，以便我方可以在 7 月发货。
10. 由于港口拥挤，请将装运日期和信用证的有效期分别延长至 3 月 31 日及 4 月 15 日。

Ⅲ. Please translate the following letter into English.

敬启者：

我们已收到由也门建设与发展银行开立的金额为 13720 美元的有关 16000 打弹力尼龙袜的第 154、88 信用证。审核后，我们发现不允许转船和分运。

由于你港的直达船稀少，我们不得不经常在香港转船。至于分运，把手头的货马上运出而不是等整批货一起运是符合我们双方的利益的。

因此，我们今天下午传真你方请求修改信用证如下："允许转船和分运"如你方能设法尽快电改，我们将非常高兴，因为货物已备妥多时。

致礼！

Ⅳ. Extensive reading.

WTO Encourage Development and Economic Reform

Over the past 60 years, the WTO, which was established in 1995, and its predecessor organization the GATT have helped to create a strong and prosperous international trading system, thereby contributing to unprecedented global economic growth. The WTO currently has 164 members, of which 117 are developing countries or separate customs territories. WTO activities are supported by a Secretariat of some 700 staff, led by the WTO Director-General. The Secretariat is located in Geneva, Switzerland, and has an annual budget of approximately CHF 200 million ($180 million, €130 million). The three official languages of the WTO are English, French and Spanish.

The overall objective of the WTO is to help its members use trade as a means to raise living standards, create jobs and improve people's lives. The WTO operates the global system of trade rules and helps developing countries build their trade capacity. It also provides a forum for its members to negotiate trade agreements and to resolve the trade problems they face with each other. The WTO agreements are lengthy and complex because they are legal texts covering a wide range of activities. They deal with: agriculture, textiles and clothing, banking, telecommunications, government purchases, industrial standards and product safety, food sanitation regulations, intellectual property, and much more. But a number of simple, fundamental principles run throughout all of these documents. These principles are the foundation of the multilateral trading system.

The WTO system contributes to development. Developing countries need flexibility in the time they take to implement the system's agreements. And the agreements themselves inherit the earlier provisions of GATT that allow for special assistance and trade concessions for developing countries.

Over three quarters of WTO members are developing countries and countries in transition to market economies. During the seven and a half years of the Uruguay Round, over 60 of these countries implemented trade liberalization programs autonomously. At the same time, developing countries and transition economies were much more active and influential in the Uruguay Round negotiations than in any previous round, and they are even more so in the current Doha Development Agenda.

At the end of the Uruguay Round, developing countries were prepared to take on most of the obligations that are required of developed countries. But the agreements did give them transition periods to adjust to the more unfamiliar and, perhaps, difficult WTO provisions — particularly so for the poorest, "least-developed" countries. A ministerial decision adopted at the end of the round says better-off countries should accelerate implementing market access commitments on goods exported by the least-developed countries, and it seeks increased technical assistance for them. More recently, developed countries have started to allow duty-free and quota-free imports for almost all products from least-developed countries. On all of this, the WTO and its members are still going through a learning process. The current Doha Development Agenda includes developing countries' concerns about the difficulties they face in implementing the Uruguay Round agreements.

Please complete the following tasks.

Task 1. Questions
(1) What's the World Trade Organization?
(2) What does WTO do?
(3) How does WTO help the developing countries to improve their trade and economy?

Task 2. Group Discussion
What are the advantages and disadvantages of China entering into WTO?

V. Comprehensive documents filling.

Part One
Direction: Please read the following L/C and the additional information, then complete the commercial invoice and Certificate of Origin.

LETTER OF CREDIT

SEQUENCE OF TOTAL	*27	1 / 1
FORM OF DOC, CREDIT	*40A	IRREVOCABLE
DOC. CREDIT NUMBER	*20	7877876
DATE OF ISSUE	31C	160115 (YY-MM-DD)
DATE AND PLACE OF EXPIRY	*31D	DATE 160310 PLACE IN THE COUNTRY OF BENEFICIARY
APPLICANT	*50	SAKULA CORPORATION 6-7, KAWARA MACH OSAKA, JAPAN
ISSUING BANK	52A	FUJI BANK LTD 156, OTOLIKINGZA MACHI TOKYO, JAPAN
BENEFICIARY	*59	SHANGHAI IMPORT & EXPORT LTD. CORPORATION, 166 HONGKOU ROAD, SHANGHAI, CHINA
AMOUNT	*32B	CURRENCY USD AMOUNT 18,500.00
AVAILABLE WITH/BY	*41D	ANY BANK IN CHINA BY NEGOTIATION
DRAFTS AT	42C	DRAFTS AT SIGHT FOR FULL INVOICE COST
DRAWEE	42A	FUJI BANK LTD
PARTIAL SHIPMENTS	43P	PROHIBITED
TRANSSHIPMENT	43T	ALLOWED
LOADING ON BOARD	44A	SHANGHAI
FOR TRANSPORTATION TO…	44B	OSAKA PORT
LATEST DATE OF SHIPMENT	44C	160216
DESCRIPT OF GOODS	45A	COTTON BLANKET ART NO.H46 300 PCS USD 5.50/PC ART NO.H56 300 PCS USD 4.50/PC ART NO.H66 300 PCS USD 4.80/PC ART NO.H76 300 PCS USD 5.20/PC ART NO.H86 300 PCS USD 5.00/PC CIF OSAKA
DOCUMENTS REQUIRED	46A	+ SIGNED COMMERCIAL INVOICE IN TRIPLICATE. + PACKING LIST IN TRIPLICATE IN TRIPLICATE. + CERTIFICATE OF ORIGIN GSP CHINA FORM A, ISSUED BY THE CHAMBER OF COMMERCE OR OTHER AUTHORITY DULY ENTITLED FOR THIS PURPOSE. + 3/3 SET OF CLEAN ON BOARD OCEAN BILLS OF LADING, MADE OUT TO ORDER OF SHIPPER AND BLANK ENDORSED AND MARKED "FREIGHT PREPAID " AND NOTIFY APPLICANT. + FULL SET OF NEGOTIABLE INSURANCE POLICY OR

CHARGES	71B	CERTIFICATE BLANK ENDORSED FOR 110 PCT OF INVOICE VALUE COVERING ALL RISKS. ALL BANKING CHARGES OUTSIDE JAPAN ARE FOR ACCOUNT OF BENEFICIARY.
PERIOD FOR PRESENTATION	48	DOCUMENTS MUST BE PRESENTED WITHIN 15 DAYS AFTER THE DATE OF SHIPMENT BUT WITHIN THE VALIDITY OF THE CREDIT.

Additional Information:

(1) INVOICE NO: BCC12456

(2) INVOICE DATE: FEB 17th, 2016

(3) PACKING

G.W: 20.5KGS/CTN N.W: 20.0KGS/CTN MEAS: 0.2CBM/CTN

PACKED IN 250 CARTONS

PACKED IN TWO 20' CONTAINER（集装箱号: TEXU2263999; TEXU2264000）

(4) HS. CODE: 5802.3090

(5) VESSEL: XINGHUA V.086

(6) B/L NO: EDDS0511861

(7) B/L DATE: FEB 16th, 2016

SHANG HAI IMPORT & EXPORT LTD. CORPORATION

166 HONGKOU ROAD, SHANGHAI, CHINA

COMMERCIAL INVOICE

TEL: 021-65788877   INV NO: __(1)__

FAX: 021-65788876   DATE: Feb. 17th, 2016

FROM: Shanghai   TO: __(2)__

MARKS & NO	DESCRIPTIONS OF GOODS	QUANTITY	U/ PRICE	AMOUNT
	(3)	300PCS 300PCS 300PCS 300PCS 300PCS	(4)	USD 18,500.00

TOTAL AMOUNT: __(5)__

WE HEREBY CERTIFY THAT THE CONTENTS OF INVOICE HEREIN ARE TRUE AND CORRECT.

SHANGHAI IMPORT & EXPORT TRADE CORPORATION

1.Goods consigned from (Exporter's business name, address, country) SHANGHAI IMPORT & EXPORT LTD. CORPORATION, 166 HONGKOU ROAD, SHANGHAI, CHINA	Reference No.: **GENERALIZED SYSTEM OF PREFERENCES** **CERTIFICATE OF ORIGIN** **(COMBINED DECLARATION AND CERTIFICATE)**

2. Goods consigned to (Consignee's name, address, country)			FORM A		
(6)			ISSUED IN THE PEOPLE'S REPUBLIC OF CHINA (COUNTRY)		
3.Means of transport and route (as far as known)			SEE NOTES OVERLEAF		
(7)			4.For official use		
5.Item number (8)	6.Marks and numbers of packages	7.Number and kind of packages; description of goods (9)	8. Origin criterion (see notes overleaf) P	9.Gross weight or other quantity (10)	10. Number and date of invoices. BCC12456, FEB 17th, 2016
11.Certification It is hereby certified, on the basis of control carried out, that the declaration by the exporter is correct. ------ Place and date, signature and stamp of certifying authority			12.Declaration by the exporter The undersigned hereby declares that the above details and statements are correct; that all the goods were produced in **CHINA** (country) and that they comply with the origin requirements specified for those goods in the Generalized System of Preference for goods exported to (importing country) ------ Place and date, signature of authorized signatory.		

(1) _____
(2) _____
(3) _____
(4) _____
(5) _____
(6) _____
(7) _____
(8) _____
(9) _____
(10) _____

Part Two

Directions: Please read the following documents and find 5 discrepancies based on the L/C and additional information.

BILL OF LADING

Shipper SHANHAI IMPORT & EXPORT CORPORATION 168 HONGKOU ROAD, SHANGHAI, CHINA		B/L NO. COCS0511860 ***ORIGINAL*** 中国对外贸易运输总公司 CHINA NATIONAL FOREIGN TRADE TRANSPORT	
Consignee or order **TO ORDER**		CORPORATION 直运或转船提单	
Notify address SAKULA CORPORATION 6-7 KAWARA OSAKA JAPAN		BILL OF LADING DIRECT OR WITH TRANSHIPMENT	
		SHIPPED on board in apparent good order and condition (unless otherwise indicated) the goods or packages specified herein and to be discharged or the mentioned port of discharge of as near there as the vessel may safely get and be always afloat.	
Pre-carriage by	Port of loading SHANGHAI	THE WEIGHT, measure, marks and numbers quality, contents and value, being particularly furnished by the Shipper, are not checked by the Carrier on loading.	
Vessel NANXING V.086	Port of transshipment		
Port of discharge OSAKA	Frail destination	THE SHIPPER, Consignee and the Holder of this Bill of Lading hereby expressly accept and agree to all printed, written or stamped provisions, exceptions and conditions of this Bill of Loading, including those on the back hereof. IN WITNESS where of the number of original Bill of Loading stated below have been signed, one of which being accomplished, the other(s) to be void.	
Container/Seal No. Marks and NOS.	Number and kind of packages Designation of goods	Gross weight (kgs.)	Measurement (m^3)
T.C OSAKA C/NO.1-250	COTTON BLANKET TWO HUNDRED FIFTY (250) CARTONS ONLY TOTAL ONE 20' CONTAINER CY TO CY FREIGHT PREPAID	5,125 KGS **ON BOARD**	50CBM
REGARDING TRANSHIPMENT INFORMATION PLEASE CONTACT		Freight and charge FREIGHT PREPAID	
Ex. rate	Prepaid at	Freight payable at SHANGHAI	Place and date of issue SHANGHAI FEB 16th, 2016
	Total Prepaid	Number of original Bs/L TWO	Signed for or on behalf of the Master 李明 as Agent

Chapter 6 Packing

Task Driven

South Africa Sprout International Corporation asked Fujian Mushroom Import & Export Co., Ltd. to prepare to pack the fungi products with recyclable packaging materials. Please work in groups to design a green packaging bag to pack the fungi products.

Learning Objectives

- **Knowledge objectives:** Tell the difference among shipping marks, indicative marks and warning marks; Clarify the classification of packing.
- **Skill objectives:** Draft an email discussing packing in a proper way.
- **Affective objectives:** Develop ecological ethics of green package.

Core Concept

6.1 Importance of Packing

There are a wide range of requirements for the packing of different types of goods in terms of their sorts, natures, features and shapes. Except from those in bulk and nude cargo, a vast majority of goods are properly packed as agreed upon in the sales contract. Three reasons are given for goods to be packed correctly before they are shipped and distributed. One is that it is merely properly packed products that are typically likely to enter the fields of distribution and consumption. The packing is helpful to have the goods in good shape and to keep them intact in quantity. Secondly, it is simple and convenient to have the packed goods shipped, loaded, unloaded, stored, kept or displayed. Goods with the right packing are less likely to be lost, damaged, or stolen in transit. The third reason is that improved packing is favorable to increasing sales and strengthening competition against rivals. Products with the right and attractive packing are more favored and sought by customers than those without.

6.2 Classification of Packing

For the sake of different functions that packing performs in transit, there are typically transport packing and sales packing. The former is also referred to as large packing or outer packing, which is literally useful for transportation in terms of safety and integrity.

Transport packing can be further classified into different categories according to different attributes. The most common packing is the one which is defined in terms of shape or size, such as carton, box, crate, container, wooden case, bag, carboy, sack, drum, can, bale, pallet or bundle. As to transport packing, you can always find Shipping Mark, Indicative or handling Mark, and Warning Mark on the surface of the packaging, which are often used to identify goods, direct or warn people involved.

Unlike transport packing, the latter is also called small packing, inner packing or immediate packing, which goes with the products to reach retailers and consumers. As to sales packing, you can always find some necessary prints on it, such as trade mark, brand, name, origin, quantity, specifications, elements, functions, usage and bar code.

In addition to transport and sales packing, there may be neutral packing in actual international transactions. Neutral packing happens when the name of country, place, and manufacturer, trade mark and even brand are by no means marked and printed for particular purposes. Neutral packing is usually preferred when an exporter intends to deal with tariff barriers or non-tariff barriers and penetrate the import country in order to meet particular trading needs, for instance, entrepot trade.

The following are some packing containers:

(1) Wooden case: Made of wood, sometimes using materials such as metal bands or wires around the case—for instruments, parts, medicines (Fig. 6-1).

(2) Chest (CST, CSTS): Tin lined or water-proof paper lined—for tea and matches (Fig. 6-2).

(3) Crate(CT, CTS): A case made of wooden slates, but one not fully enclosed. It has a bottom and a frame, usually open at the top—for machinery and glass plates (Fig. 6-3).

(4) Carton(CTN, CTNS): Made of strong cardboard—for plastics, milk powder, textiles, sundry goods, and fruits (Fig. 6-4).

(5) Gunny Bag/Sack: Made of jute—for flour, grain, beans, wheat, fertilizer, and some other loose materials (Fig. 6-5).

(6) Bale (B/-, BLS)/Bundles: A package of soft goods, e.g. cotton, wool, sheepskin, tightly pressed together and maybe strengthened by metal bands and others (Fig. 6-6).

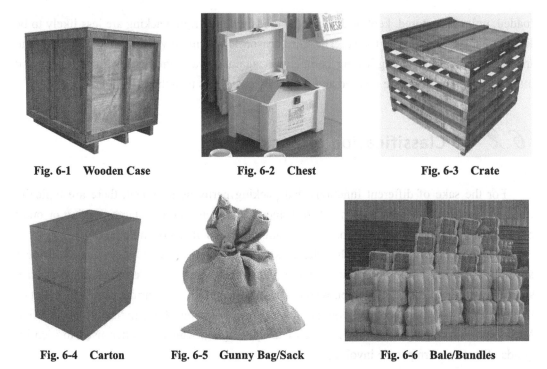

Fig. 6-1 Wooden Case   Fig. 6-2 Chest   Fig. 6-3 Crate

Fig. 6-4 Carton   Fig. 6-5 Gunny Bag/Sack   Fig. 6-6 Bale/Bundles

(7) Cask(CK, CKS)/Barrel/Drum: Including wooden drum, iron drum and plastic cask—for the conveyance of liquid or greasy and powdered goods such as beer, soy sauce, oil, dyes and chemicals (Fig. 6-7).

(8) Pallet: A large tray or platform for moving cargo in loads (Fig. 6-8).

(9) Container: A large metal box for transport (Fig. 6-9).

Fig. 6-7 Cask   Fig. 6-8 Pallet   Fig. 6-9 Container

6.3 Marking

Marking refers to different diagrams, words and figures which are written, printed or brushed on the outside of the shipping packages. There are three types of marking on export packages: shipping mark, indicative mark and warning mark.

Shipping mark is composed of a geometric figure, a simple code or initials, which will facilitate the identification and count of goods in the process of loading and unloading, shipping, and storing. The UN has recommended a type of standard shipping mark including the following four parts (Fig. 6-10):

(1) initials of the consignee's name;

(2) reference number, such as order number, or invoice number;

(3) name of port/place of destination;

(4) case number.

Indicative mark is a caution mark, which reminds people of carefulness in handling or carrying goods (Fig.6-11). It is composed of graphs and words as follows:

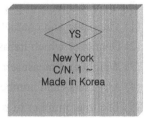

Fig. 6-10 A Sample of Shipping Mark

(1) THIS SIDE UP;

(2) FRAGILE;

(3) STOW AWAY FROM HEAT;

(4) USE NO HOOKS;

(5) TO BE KEPT COOL;

(6) DO NOT DROP;

(7) GLASS WITH CARE/HANDLE WITH CARE;

(8) PERISHABLE;

(9) KEEP DRY;

(10) DO NOT STOW ON DECK.

Warning mark is also called dangerous mark and is used to indicate explosive, poisonous, inflammable, and perishable goods (Fig. 6-12).

Fig.6-11 A Sample of Indicative Mark

Fig. 6-12 A Sample of Warning Mark

6.4 Packing list

A packing list is not required by customs in most countries, but it is an important document in the export process. The packing list may be used by the freight forwarder to prepare a bill of lading for the ocean and to understand how much room is needed for the cargo. It may be used by banks as a supporting document presented for payment under a L/C or other payment terms. It may be used by the U.S. Customs as well as by customs in the country of import for compliance and duty liability.

The main contents of packing list may include:

(1) The name and contact information of the exporter and ultimate consignee;

(2) Details of which items appear in each of the packing container;

(3) Weight and measurements of each packing container;

(4) Any marks and numbers including a container number and seal number if appropriate;

(5) The total number of pieces, weight, and measures of the entire shipment;

(6) Any special instruction or additional information that is important for the shipment.

Note: You can refer to Appendix Two for the sample of packing list.

A Letter for Requesting the Packing Details.

Sub: Re: Shipping for Order XBA226AR

Dear Susan,

Further to our email on 22 regarding the packing of the above order for Smart Choice, we would like to propose the following requirements:

(1) Our clients would like to have the products packed in window packing for inner packing so that the products can be seen directly. They believe it will help to promote sales.

(2) They prefer wooden cases to cartons for outer packing. They fear that cartons are not strong enough for ocean transportation. They might be easily damaged through rough handling. They are more susceptible to pilferage and damage by moisture.

(3) Please indicate "HANDLE WITH CARE" and mark our initials "KLQ" in triangle, under which the port of destination and our Order No. should be stenciled on the outer packing.

Please let us know if you can do as requested.

Yours faithfully,

Jefferson

Language Points

Words and Expressions

neutral packing	中性包装
designated packing	指定包装
nude packing	裸包装
rate of breakage	破损率
plastic lining	塑料衬里
stuffing material	填充材料
wooden crate	木条箱
corrugated carton	瓦楞纸箱
plywood case	胶合板箱
kraft paper bag	牛皮纸袋
carboy	大玻璃瓶
gunny bag	麻布袋
veneer case	薄板箱
barrel	琵琶桶
jute bag	麻袋
paper bag	纸袋
carton	纸板箱
pallet	托盘
wooden drum	木桶
wood shavings	刨花
sack	袋
bale	包
in bulk	散装
in block	块装
in slice	片装
in spear	条装
in bundle	捆装
packing list	装箱单
packing capacity	包装容量
packing intact	包装完整
transport packing/outer/large packing	运输（外）包装
sales packing /inner/immediate/small packing	销售（内）包装
regular packing for export	正规出口包装
in apparent good order and condition	表面状况良好
packing stained and old	包装残旧玷污

cartons wet and stained	箱遭水渍
THIS SIDE UP	此面向上
HANDLE WITH CARE	小心轻放
KEEP DRY	保持干燥
KEEP IN COOL PLACE	阴冷处储存
OPEN HERE	此处打开
TO BE KEPT UPRIGHT	竖立安放
NOT TO BE THROWN DOWN	不可抛掷
NOT TO BE TIPPED	请勿倒置
GUARD AGAINST DAMP	勿使受潮
NOT TO BE LAID FLAT	切勿平放
INFLAMMABLE	易燃货物
FRAGILE	当心破碎
EXPLOSIVES	易爆货物

Sentences

1. Folding chairs are packed 2 pieces to a carton.
两把折叠椅装一个纸板箱。

2. Each pair of nylon socks is packed in a polybag and 10 pairs to a box.
每双尼龙袜装一个塑料袋，10双装一盒。

3. The goods are packed five pieces to a carton.
货物每5件装一个纸箱。

4. The wheat is to be packed in new gunny bags of 100kg. And each bag weighs about 1.5kg.
小麦用新麻袋包装，每袋装100千克，袋重1.5千克。

5. In view of precaution, please mark "Fragile" and "Handle with care" on the outer packing.
为预防起见，请在外包装上注明"易碎"和"小心轻放"的字样。

6. The goods you packed in wooden cases are susceptible to damage by moisture.
装在木箱中的这批货物容易受潮损坏。

7. Perishable goods are subject to damage in transit.
易腐烂的货物在运输途中易损坏。

8. Please ship the above order in foam-lined boxes.
上述货物使用内部衬有泡沫塑料的木箱装运。

9. We hope that you will take measures to reinforce this sort of carton with iron straps.
我们希望你们采取措施用金属条加固这种纸板箱。

10. We intend to switch from carton packing to foil wrapping.
我们想把纸板箱包装改为金属箔材料包装

11. We pack our shirts in plastic-lined, waterproof cartons, reinforced with metal straps.
我们将衬衫包装在塑料做内衬的防水的纸箱内，并且用金属条加固。

12. The continued increase in freight costs forces us to seek improved packing methods. Could you suggest a more economical packing method for our products?

不断上涨的运费迫使我们寻求改进包装的方法。贵方能给我方建议一种更加经济的包装方式吗？

13. In addition to the production of standard packing material, we also engage in customized and special packing.

除生产标准包装材料外，我们还进行定制化包装和特殊类型包装。

14. As far as the outer packing is concerned, we will pack the goods 10 dozens to a carton, with the gross weight around 25kg a carton.

关于外包装，我方打算将货物 10 打装一个纸板箱，毛重 25 千克。

15. When you pack, please put 2 or 3 different designs and colors in each box.

每个箱子在包装时请放置 2 到 3 种不同的样式和颜色。

16. The dimensions of the carton are 40cm long, 20cm wide and 30cm high with a volume of about $0.024m^3$. The gross weight is 25kg while the net weight is 24kg.

纸箱长 40 厘米、宽 20 厘米、高 30 厘米，容积 0.024 立方米，毛重 25 千克、净重 24 千克。

17. The recycle mark must be printed in black ink on all polybags and outer cartons.

回收标志必须用黑色油墨印刷在所有塑料袋和纸箱外部。

18. The cartons are well protected against moisture by polythene sheet lining.

纸板箱里有塑料布衬里，有很好的防潮效果。

19. Each carton is lined with a water-proof material and secured by strapping, preventing contents from damage through rough handling.

每个纸箱内衬防水材料，用捆扎带加固，防止货物由于粗鲁装卸受损。

20. Regarding shipping marks, please stencil our initials in a circle.

关于唛头，请将我公司名字缩写刻成圆圈。

21. The packing and marking shall be at seller's option.

包装和唛头由卖方决定。

22. I'm afraid cardboard boxes are not strong enough for the transport by sea.

恐怕纸板箱不够结实，不适合海洋运输。

23. In order to reduce damage in transit to a minimum, we suggest that the packing of the goods should be in wooden cases.

为将损失降至最小，我方建议货物用木箱装。

24. The contract stipulates that the packing should be strong enough to withstand rough handling.

合同规定包装务必结实，可经受野蛮装卸。

25. Improving the package of the goods can further promote the sales of our products.

改进包装能进一步扩大产品的销售。

Case One

E-mail 1: from the buyer to the seller

Dear Jenny,

I'm sending you the new purchase order of Ganoderma Capsules. Please have a look at the attached files.

In this order, we need information about the label the same as last time but darken the color more than last time. Please send me the design before you make it.

Thank you so much.

David

E-mail 2: from the seller to the buyer

Dear David,

Please kindly check the attached old label design with light color.

Waiting for your reply.

Best Regards,

Jenny

E-mail 3: from the buyer to the seller

Dear Jenny,

Thank you for your support and nice suggestions.

I'm sending you a new label with the color we need and a new Halal and JAS design for you. Please see attached files.

Have a good evening.

David

Case One Analysis

Business practice

In emails about products' packing, the buyer and seller generally deal with issues such as the packing container, packing material, number of packages, shipping marks, cost of packing, packing list, etc. In this case, Jenny exchanged emails with David to negotiate the packing terms. Jenny needed to confirm the packing design with David before putting the order into production. It is necessary for them to specify the detailed packing terms in order to avoid possible trade disputes.

Packing consists of the outer packing and inner packing. The outer packing is to protect the goods against damage and theft in transportation, while the inner packing is aimed to promote sales. In this business deal, the goods were agricultural products, and the buyer and seller focused their negotiation on the inner packing. When placing an order, David (the buyer) requested information about the label used in the last deal, and asked for a slight change in color. In reply, Jenny (the seller) sent the old label design for the buyer's reference. In the third email, David attached the newly revised label design, as well as Halal and JAS design, so that the seller can prepare the production and packing as required.

Writing strategy

These emails are organized as follows:

(1) To mention the purchase order, and request information about the label (email from the buyer);

(2) To reply and send the old label design (email from the seller);

(3) To express thanks and specify the new requirement for the label and logo (email from the buyer).

Business terms

(1) Halal logo: The Halal certificate is a document that guarantees that products and services aimed at the Muslim population meet the requirements of Islamic law and therefore are suitable for consumption in both Muslim-majority countries and in Western countries where there are significant population groups who practice Islam. Halal certification is a process which ensures the features and quality of products according to the rules established by the Islamic Council that allows the use of the Halal mark. It is mainly applied to meat products and other food products such as milk, canned food and additives. Products that are Halal certified are often marked with a Halal logo.

(2) JAS Logo: Japanese Agricultural Standards, abbreviated as JAS, are the Japanese national standards in the field of agricultural, forestry, fisheries, and food industry. The general JAS logo is applied to foods and forestry products which conform to the JAS quality, for example, quality grade, composition and specification.

Case Two

E-mail 1: from the buyer to seller

Dear Jenny,

For future ingredient shipment, please ensure all the packaging label indicate the information below:

(1) Material name (must be the same as in Halal cert/Spec/MSDS/COA provided);
(2) Manufacturer's Name and full company address (must be the same information as stated in Halal cert);
(3) Batch number;
(4) Shelf life;
(5) Manufacturing date;
(6) Expiration date;
(7) Quantity.

Regards,

David

E-mail 2: from the seller to buyer

Dear David,

Good day.

Based on your requirements, enclosed is the label and shipping mark for your reference, which refer to the information of Halal certificate. Please kindly confirm them. Thanks in advance.

Well note that the product name of COA, MSDS, and all original documents for customs clearance will refer to the information of Halal certificate. I will provide all documents copy for your reference before the shipment.

Thank you.
Best regards,

Jenny

E-mail 3: from the buyer to the seller

Dear Jenny,

Good morning. Here to confirm that the label format is correct.

Thanks for your fast action.

Regards,

David

Case Two Analysis

Business practice

In this case, the buyer and the seller have not closed any business deals before this transaction. Hence, David (the buyer) gave a detailed requirement for the packaging label. The packaging label, as an important part of inner packaging, involves specific information of the goods, such as material name, manufacture's name and company address, batch number, shelf life, manufacturing date, expiration date and quantity. The reason why David placed an emphasis on the inner packing was that good inner packing could save cost and time in marketing and help to promote sales.

In reply, Jenny sent the label and shipping marks according to the buyer's request. Shipping marks are generally stenciled on the outer packaging, the purpose of which is to identify the goods, and facilitate transportation, handling and storage. The shipping marks usually include such information as initials of the buyer, contract number, destination port, number of packages, origin of the goods, weight and dimensions of packages, etc..

Note: batch number (生产批次号), shelf life (保质期), manufacturing date (生产日期)

Writing strategy

These emails are organized as follows:

(1) To inform the other party of the packing requirements, particularly the packaging label (email from the buyer);

(2) To mention the attachments relevant to the packing method, such as label, logo and shipping marks (email from the seller);

(3) To confirm the label format and express thanks (email from the buyer).

Business terms

(1) COA: Certificate of Analysis (COA) refers to a document from a supplier that states the identity, purity, or microbiological state of a product. It shows that the supplier has completed the required testing and the result meets the product specifications.

(2) MSDS: Material Safety Data Sheet, abbreviated as MSDS, is a safety document that manufacturers provide with their products. The document generally includes information related to the safe use and storage of the product, such as its physical properties, chemical properties, and emergency control measures.

Skills Training

I. Choose the best answer.

1. All the products are _____ first quality.
   A. for	B. at	C. of	D. with
2. _____ please find our price list.
   A. Enclose	B. Enclosed	C. Enclosing	D. Be enclosed
3. We hope that you will dispatch the goods_____ us before August 15th.
   A. reach	B. to reach	C. reached	D. reaching
4. We would appreciate it if you could let us have an ample_____ of samples for free distribution.
   A. supply	B. quantity	C. amount	D. sum
5. _____ we would like to help you, there is no room for earlier shipment.
   A. Much as	B. Much	C. Even	D. As
6. I wonder if it is possible for you to _____ shipment in March.
   A. do	B. arrange	C. fix	D. effect
7. Our strong packaging will certainly help_____ the sales of the product.
   A. promotional	B. promotion	C. promote	D. promoting
8. It was found upon examination that nearly 20% of the _____ has been broken, obviously due to improper_____.
   A. packing, packages	B. packages, packing
   C. packing, packing	D. packages, packages
9. The overall_____ of the case are 100cm×50cm×50cm.
   A. volumes	B. weights	C. capacities	D. dimensions
10. Each pair of Nylon Socks is packed_____ a polybag and 12 pairs_____ a box.
    A. in, to	B. in, with	C. to, in	D. with, to

II. Translation.

Part One

Direction: Translate the following sentences into Chinese.

1. Each set is wrapped in a polybag and packed in a standard export carton lined with foam.

2. Packing list should be in duplicate, indicating gross weight, net weight, measurements and quantity of the package.

3. The goods must be packed in seaworthy export cases, suitable for long distance ocean transportation and capable of withstanding rough handling.

4. Please see to it that indicative marks like "FRAGILE" and "HANDLE WITH CARE" should be stenciled on the outer packing.

5. Please mark our initials in a rectangle, under which are the quantity and port of destination.

Part Two

Direction: Translate the following sentences into English.

6. 发动机部件应使用防水材料包裹并装在板条箱中。
7. 由于茶具容易破损，因此应使用柔软的材料包裹并牢固地包装在纸板箱中。
8. 我们可以满足贵方对包装的特殊要求，但额外费用应由贵方承担。
9. 每个木箱的尺寸和重量应清晰地印刷在箱体上，并注明木箱编号，以便于识别。
10. 为了消除未来可能遇到的麻烦，我方希望事先明确我们的包装要求。

Ⅲ. Fill in the blanks with appropriate words.

1. Packing in cardboard box_____a little bit of flower designs is suitable_____display in supermarket.

2. The cardboard boxes are not strong enough_____the transport by sea.

3. In order to reduce damage_____transit to a minimum, we suggest that the packing of the goods should be_____wooden cases.

4. We request shipment to be made by 2 equal lots_____an interval of 10 days.

5. We can arrange multi-modal combined transport_____rail and sea.

6. Our products are packed in cartons lined_____poly sheet.

7. Most_____our clients took our cartons as being strong enough_____withstand ocean transportation.

8. In view of precaution, please mark "FRAGILE" and "HANDLE WITH CARE"_____the outer packing.

9. For the sake of precaution, the cartons must be secured_____metal bands.

10. These cartons are well protected_____moisture by plastic lining.

Ⅳ. Extensive reading.

Since the 20th century, when people are faced with various problems brought by the industrial civilization, especially environmental pollution and ecological crisis, they have to reflect on the production, lifestyle and values of industrial civilization, and turn their hope to a new civilization-ecological civilization, which pursues the harmonious unity and coordinated development of man and nature. The construction of ecological civilization in the new era lays the emphasis on the harmony between man and nature, man and man, and man and himself as its core value, which coincides with the concept of harmony or "He" in Chinese traditional culture. It can be said that it is the rational sublimation of the philosophical concept of harmony under the new historical conditions.

In an increasingly connected world fraught with grave challenges, the wisdom of harmony sheds light on how humanity can create a prosperous and peaceful future in a sustainable, environmentally friendly and cooperative way. It provides profound theoretical foundation and ideological enlightenment for the settlement of the conflict between man and nature in ecological civilization. People take the thought of "unity of heaven and man" as a harmonious model to deal with the relationship between man and nature. On one hand, it emphasizes that man and nature should be regarded as a complete and harmonious whole, and that there should be an interdependent relationship between man and nature. On the other hand, it highlights the particularity of human beings compared with other things, positions the relationship between man and nature in a positively coordinated relationship, and advocates that human beings should shoulder the responsibility of protecting nature and other creatures, instead of blindly conquering nature. Therefore, the ecological civilization on the basis of the traditional concept of harmony differs from sustainable development in the emphasis placed on political and cultural factors, but defines new relationships between man and nature that would permit living well and within the eco-environmental bounds of planet Earth.

The green package, also known as pollution-free package and environmental friendly package, refers to the package that is harmless to the ecological environment and human health, can be reused and regenerated, and conforms to the sustainable development. The pursuit of green packages has been highlighted in international trade, which means that packages should be simple, applicable and beautiful as well as harmless to the environment. From the development and design of packaging materials to the recycling of packaging waste, the entire process minimizes environmental pollution, effectively circulates green packaging materials, and meets the requirements of ecological system balance. Accordingly, the construction of ecological civilization in China will inevitably lead to the "green reform" of the packaging industry. It is conductive to build the ecological ethics of green packaging and guide entrepreneurs moving from the traditional packaging industry to the path of transformation and upgrading for achieving both economic and environmental development.

Questions.
(1) What is green packages?
(2) What are the functions of green packages?
(3) What is the relationship among harmony, environmental civilization and green packages?

V. Group work.

(1) Please work in groups to design a green packaging bag to pack the fungi products.
(2) Peer evaluation.
Have a group discussion to evaluate the package every group has designed and decide which group performs the best based on the principle of safety (materials, transportation environment), cost (low cost but proper packing) and beauty (appearance, design and philosophy).

Chapter 7 Shipment

Task Driven

Due to the urgent need of fungi products from South Africa Sprout International Corporation, Fujian Mushroom Import & Export Co. Ltd. sent the cargo by air. The air freight prices for general cargo from Fuzhou to Cape Town are as follows:

DHL	TNT
First 500g: RMB 280	First 500g: RMB 300
Refill 500g: RMB 60	Refill 500g: RMB 75
Fuel: 11.25%	Fuel: 11%
Timing: 5～7 working days	Timing: 4～5 working days

Both ways arrive in Cape Town in approximately one week.

Please write a shipping notice to South Africa Sprout International Corporation based on the above information, confirming the mode of transportation, freight information, arrival time and so forth.

Learning Objectives

• **Knowledge objectives:** Be familiar with various modes of transportation and their pros & cons; Understand the importance of Bill of Lading.

• **Skill objectives:** Be able to write letters to rush shipment or discuss shipping details.

• **Affective objectives:** Realize the impact of transportation such as China's high-speed rail development on international trade.

Core Concept

7.1 Introduction

In international trade, shipment is an important link in the process of contract performance. It refers to the carriage of the goods from the exporter to the importer. The carrier can be liner or tramp. If the transaction is concluded on CIF or CFR basis, the seller is responsible for space booking, while on FOB basis, the responsibility shall be borne by the buyer.

The procedure of shipment includes giving shipping instructions by buyers, confirming the shipping rate, appointing a shipping agent or carrier, booking shipping space or chartering ships, making customs declaration, arranging shipment, sending shipping advice by sellers, etc. Much of the work in this procedure is usually handled by professional shipping and forwarding agent.

7.2 Bill of Lading

A Bill of lading is a transportation document which is issued by an ocean carrier to a shipper with whom the carrier has entered into a contract for the carriage of goods. The B/L is normally made out in 3 sets, including three features: receipt of the goods, evidence of the contract of carriage, and document of the title to the goods.

7.3 Letters of Shipment

Letters on shipment are usually written for the following intentions: to rush an early shipment; to amend shipping terms (request for transshipment and partial shipment); to send shipping advice; to present shipping documents and so on.

A letter of Shipping Advice/Instruction usually includes the following contents:

(1) The date and number of B/L;
(2) The date and number of the contract;
(3) The name of commodities and their quality and value;
(4) The number of packages and total quantity;
(5) The name of the carrying vessel;
(6) The name of the loading port;
(7) The estimated time of departure (ETD);

(8) The name of the destination port;

(9) The estimated time of arrival (ETA);

(10) Negotiable draft or not;

(11) Providing relevant shipping documents (Copies).

Letters on urging shipment or allowing partial shipments/transshipment usually cover the following points:

(12) Identify references;

(13) Reasons for urging shipment or allowing partial shipment/transshipment;

(14) Your expectations.

7.4 Supplementary Materials about Shipping Companies

Top 10   International Container Shipping Companies

Company	Number of Ships	Market Share	Headquarter
Maersk Line	763	18.0%	Copenhagen Denmark
Mediterranean Shipping Company(MSC)	469	14.6%	Geneva, Switzerland
CMA-CGM	441	11.1%	Marseille, France
China Ocean Shipping (Group) Company (COSCO)	277	8.0%	Beijing, China
Hapag-Lloyd	219	5.2%	Hamburg, Germany
Evergreen	186	5.0%	Taoyuan City, Taiwan
Yang Ming	100	2.9%	Keelung, Taiwan
United Arab Shipping Company	56	2.7%	Dubai, U.A.E.
Nippon Yusen Kaisha	97	2.7%	Tokyo, Japan

Source: Wikipedia, ranked in order of capacity of fleet based on data by May 1st, 2017

7.5 Sample Letters

Sample One: Rushing the Exporter to Effect Shipment

Dear Ada,

Referring to the Contract No.3522, please let us know when we may expect delivery of "Sanyang" Brand Sewing Machines ordered one month ago. Our letter of credit opened with our bank in your favor must have reached you for quite some time. We hope that you could ship the goods, by the next steamer "Fuxing", which is due to sail from your city on or about the 15th of March to our port, as our customers are anxious to have these machines within the next month.

Please do your best and reply at your earliest convenience.

Yours faithfully,
Linda

Sample Two: Proposing Partial Shipment

Dear Sir,

Thank you for your letter of 4 May. In order to help you to recommend our products to your clients as early as possible, we agree to your proposal to advance the initial shipment for 1/3 of the total quantity from August/September to July/August. The remaining 2/3 will be shipped during August/September.

As for your request for alteration of the port of destination from Singapore to Belawan, we wish to say that the direct sailings from here to Belawan are at present few and far between. Besides, the transshipment charges are very high. Therefore it will be nice if you will comply with the original agreement for destination, so as to avoid any possible delay and extra expenses.

Your early reply will be highly appreciated.

Sincerely,
Mary

Words and Expressions

transshipment	转运
consignor	发货人
consignee	收货人
shipper	托运人
carrier	承运人
liner	班轮
tramp	不定期船
freight	运费
endorsement	背书
B/L	提单
weight	重量
quantity	数量
quality	质量
GW	毛重
NW	净重
measurement	体积
CY (Container Yard)	集装箱堆场
FCL (Full Container Load)	整箱
LCL (Less Container Load)	拼箱

forwarder	货运代理
make/effect/handle shipment	发货
expedite/rush/hasten shipment	加速发货
time of shipment	装运日期
spread shipment	分批装运
partial shipment	分批装运
port of loading	装运港
port of destination	目的港
port of unloading/discharge	卸货港
place of delivery	交货地
book shipping space	订舱位
charter transport	租船运输
container transport	集装箱运输
Ocean Bill of Lading	海运提单
clean B/L	清洁提单
straight B/L	记名提单
order B/L	指示提单
defective goods	瑕疵商品
to order	凭指示
liner transport/service	班轮运输
parcel post transport	邮包运输
measurement ton	尺码吨
perishables	易腐坏货物
prompt shipment	按时装运
sail for	驶往某目的港
sailing schedule	船期表
seal lock number	铅封号
Shipping Advice	装运通知
Shipping Instruction	装运指示
Shipping Mark	唛头
shipping space	舱位
time charter	期租船运输
timed shipment	定期装运
weight ton	重量吨
unclean/foul/claused B/L	不洁、瑕疵、批注提单
COSCO Container Lines Co., Ltd.	中远集装箱运输有限公司
APL (American President Lines)	美国总统轮船有限公司
Evergreen Marine Corporation(EMC)	长荣海运股份有限公司
Maersk Line	马士基航运公司
international multi-modal transport	国际多式联运

Sentences

1. As our traditional Spring Festival holiday is approaching, it will be difficult for us to book shipping space. To make it easier, we hope transshipment and partial shipment are allowed.
由于临近春节假期,舱位紧张,订舱将会更为困难。为便于安排订舱,我们希望允许转运和分批装运。

2. Only by the end of this month can these goods be packed ready for delivery.
这些货物只能到本月底才能包装完毕等待装运。

3. As there is no direct steamer to your port from Ningbo, the goods have to be transshipped at Shanghai.
由于没有从宁波直达你方港口的轮船,货物不得不在上海转运。

4. As the boxes are likely to receive rough handling at this end, you must see to it that packing is strong enough to protect goods.
由于货物在我处可能会遭遇粗暴搬运,所以请注意包装定要牢固以保护商品。

5. We would ask you to do everything possible to ensure punctual shipment.
我们希望你方尽一切努力保证按时装运。

6. You may rest assured that we will have the goods shipped before April 20, 2018.
请放心,我们定将于2018年4月20日前发货。

7. Please be assured that we will effect shipment in compliance with the contracted terms.
我方会按照合同约定的条款发货。

8. We have to advise you that we are unable to dispatch your order in full owing to a great shortage of shipping space.
很遗憾地通知您,由于舱位严重不足,我方无法完成一次性发货。

9. In the event of force majeure or any contingencies beyond our control, we shall not be held responsible for the late delivery or non-delivery of the goods.
当遇到不可抗力或者是不可预料的突发情况,我方对货物未能按时到达或未能到达不负责任。

10. We are pleased to inform you that the goods under your order No.216 have been dispatched today per S.S. "Dalian" scheduled to arrive at your port in the middle of May.
我们高兴地通知你们,你方第216号订单项下的货物已于今日由"大连"号轮发运,预定于5月中旬抵达你港。

11. With regard to our order No.121 of 20th August for shipment in May, we regret to have to remind you that so far we have not heard from you about the shipment and must ask you to ship the goods without delay.
关于我方8月20日第121号订单项下的货物要求在5月装运的事宜,我们不得不抱歉地提醒你方我们至今都没有接到任何装运的消息,故我们必须要求你方立即装运。

12. We have the pleasure to inform you that your Order No.316 has been shipped today per S.S. "Fuxing" from Xiamen to New York. We are sending you enclosed

invoice No.2001 for $1,900 and please note that we have drawn on you for this amount at sight for collection through the Bank of China, together with the relevant shipping documents.

我方很高兴地通知你方,第 316 号订单所订购之货已于今日由"复兴"轮自厦门运往纽约,随函附上第 2001 号的 1900 美元发票一张。请注意,我们已开出即期汇票连同有关装运单据也已通过中国银行托收。

13. Will you please inform us of the date of shipment and quantities you can supply from stock. Upon hearing from you we will place an order with you at once.

请告知装运期及能供应现货的数量,接到你方通知后,我们将立即向你方订货。

14. We are prepared to place a trial order provided that you can guarantee shipment on or before October 15th.

如果你方保证在 10 月 15 日或之前发货,我们准备向你方试订。

15. As we mentioned in our previous letter, shipment for the suits made to order is not possible in less than two months, but we would like to give your order a special priority.

如前函所述,定制的外套不可能在两个月内完成装运,但我们愿意对你方订单优先处理。

16. We are very sorry to inform you of a delay in the shipment of your order No. 812 on January 25th because of recent regulations imposed on reports to your country by our government and we have to obtain a license to execute your order. As soon as we receive it we shall effect shipment without delay.

我们抱歉地通知你方,你方 1 月 25 日第 812 号订单将延迟装运,因为我国政府最近对出口到你国的货物执行新的规程,我们必须取得许可证才能履行你方订单。一旦我们取得出口证,我们将立即装运货物绝不延迟。

17. The steamer is sailing for your port tomorrow and it is expected to arrive in 20 days.

该货轮明天起航前往你港,预计 20 天后抵达。

18. As our users are in urgent need of the consignment, please get the goods dispatched within the stipulated time.

由于我们的客户急需此批货物,请按规定的时间发货。

19. We are delighted to inform you that the goods you ordered are ready for shipment. Please let us have instructions for packing and dispatch.

我们很高兴通知你:你方订购的货物已备妥等待装运,请告知包装及装运要求。

20. Owing to the delay in opening the L/C, shipment cannot be made in June as contracted and should be postponed until July.

由于开证推迟,无法按合同要求在 6 月发货,这批货将延期到 7 月发运。

Case Study

E-mail 1: from the seller to buyer.

Hi David,

Thank you for your payment. Upon receiving the payment, we booked the shipping date on April 1st, 2022. But now the shipping date is unfixed due to exceptional cases.

Best Regards,

Jenny

E-mail 2: from the buyer to seller.

Hi Jenny

Once you have final confirmation of the date, please let us know and send us the BOL and the ISF.

Thank you!

David

E-mail 3: from the seller to buyer.

Dear David,

Please check the attached BL draft and confirm if everything is correct on the BL.

Once we get the confirmed shipping date, I will send you at once the final BL and ISF. Do not worry.

Best Regards,

Jenny

E-mail 4: from the buyer to seller.

Dear David,

Please check the attached BL draft and ISF. Kindly confirm if everything is correct on the BL and kindly make a declaration on ISF.

Thanks.

Jenny

E-mail 5: from the seller to buyer.
Hi Jenny,

Thanks for your BL. Everything is correct, and the ISF has already been done.

Have a nice day.

David

E-mail 6: from the buyer to seller.
Dear David,

Thank you so much for your confirmation.

We will update you once the shipment leave the seaport.

Jenny

Case Analysis

Business practice

Delivery involves a wide range of concerns, such as time of shipment, ports of loading and destination, means of transportation, partial shipment, transshipment, chartering vessels, issuing shipping documents, preparing customs clearance, etc. In this case, Jenny and David wrote emails to discuss issues concerning the delay of delivery date, examination of B/L and preparation for customs clearance. As the deal was concluded on CIF basis, it was Jenny's responsibility to book freight space and advise David of shipping information before delivery, so that David could arrange to take delivery of the goods. Jenny sent an email to David immediately after receiving the payment, informing him of the late delivery due to the epidemic. Afterwards, she attached the B/L draft and ISF for David's confirmation. B/L, issued by the shipping company, provides a testimony to the fact that the goods have been received by the shipping company, as well as the title to the goods. ISF is used to declare specific data of imported goods to the customs. When the goods were to be shipped on board, Jenny would be expected to send shipping advice to David, which might include such information as the contract number, the name of commodity, the number of packages, the total quantity, the name of vessel, the sailing date, and the total amount of the goods.

Writing strategy

The emails are organized as follows:

(1) To mention the information about delivery date;
(2) To explain the reason for late delivery;
(3) To send the buyer required shipping documents for his confirmation;
(4) To make a promise to send the shipping advice immediately after vessel's departure.

Business terms

(1) BOL: A bill of lading (B/L or BOL) is a legal document issued by a carrier to a shipper that details the type, quantity, and destination of the goods being carried. A bill of lading also serves as a shipment receipt when the carrier delivers the goods at a predetermined destination.

(2) ISF: ISF (Importer Security Filing) is a rule that obliges importing US parties to declare specific data (description of commodity) of the imported goods to the US Customs. Customs need to receive the declaration latest 24 hours prior to loading. The complete ISF must be declared 48 hours before vessel's departure out of the port of loading.

Skills Training

I. Choose the best answer.

1. We will do our best to_____shipment to meet your requirements in time.
   A. comply   B. make   C. expedite   D. arrange

2. Passenger liners often take a certain amount of_____.
   A. cargoes   B. commodity   C. shipments   D. quantities

3. We have the pleasure to inform you that the shipment has gone_____per S.S. "East Wind" and hope that it will arrive at the destination in_____condition.
   A. on, good   B. for, complete C. forward, perfect D. onto, perfect

4. The shipment time is June or July at our_____and the goods will be shipped in one _____.
   A. choice, shipment   B. option, lot
   C. decision, cargo   D. option, consignment

5. We regret our inability to_____with your request for shipping the goods in early November.
   A. compliance   B. comply   C. manage   D. arrange

6. Before deciding which form of transport to use, a_____will take into account the costs, speed and safety.
   A. insurance company   B. consignee
   C. shipper   D. shipowner

7. Any loss or damage noticed when the goods are delivered must be reported to the ____ at the time, otherwise he will not be liable for it.
   A. carrier   B. shipper   C. consignee   D. consignor

8. They intended to lower the cost of the products. _____, they did not succeed in

reducing the package costs.

    A. Therefore   B. And   C. However   D. Furthermore

9. As the_____of the goods was not strong enough to withstand the rough sea voyage, shipment was withheld at the last minute in order to give time for_____improvement.

    A. pack, packet   B. package, packing

    C. package, packaging   D. packing, packaging

10. The introduction of containers in transport greatly_____carriage of goods.

    A. facilitate   B. speeds   C. facilitates   D. economizes

Ⅱ. Complete the following sentences.

1. We shall appreciate it if you will inform us of the condition of packing as soon as the _____(当货物到达你方).

2. This is to apply to all orders_____(除非另有规定).

3. _____(由于供应商的拖延), we must ask you to extend the date of shipment from March 15th to April 10th.

4. _____ (附件是运输单) of this consignment.

5. As the only direct steamer which_____(每个月在本港口停留一次) has just departed, goods can only be shipped next month.

6. We have to advise you that we are unable to dispatch your order in full _____(由于舱位严重不足).

7. Today we_____(已发货) on board S.S. "Meller" which sails to your port tomorrow.

8. We could not _____(整批发货) on the same vessel.

9. Shipment is to be made from May to August_____(平均分为三批发货).

10. Packing of our Men's Shirts is each in a polybag, 5 dozens to _____ (纸箱有内衬防水纸,外部用铁带加固).

Ⅲ. Please translate the following letter into English.

敬启者：

贵方 4 月 20 日来函收悉，关于第 955 号购货合同下的 10,000 套梅花扳手 (Double Offset Ring Spanners)，兹函告如下：

按合同规定，上述货物应于 5 日、7 日、9 日 3 个月分 3 批等量装运。但直至目前，仍未装运第一批货物。我方客户正等此货，并为你方拖延交货而深感惊讶。

请尽力在 7 月底前把第一批货和第二批货一起装运。否则我方客户将对你方延迟装运 而深感不满，因而有可能取消订单，到别处购买。

见此函后，请告知确切装运日期。

                                                                                          谨启

IV. Extensive reading.

The Globalization of China's High-speed Railway

China's high-speed railway and its corresponding rail transportation equipment industry have become a symbol of the rapid economic development and the ongoing industrial transformation and upgrading of this ambitious resurgent nation. With high-speed rail and the expansion of its domestic industrial clusters as a solid base, China and its entrepreneurs are now ready to reach out to the international marketplace. Thanks to the unmatched quality of its high-speed rail technology, China has transformed its name into a powerful brand in exploiting oversea markets.

Phase two of the Ankara-Istanbul high-speed railway project was completed at the end of July. It connects Ankara, the capital city of Turkey, and the country's biggest city, Istanbul. The project will be of direct benefit to the Turkish people, and it represents an unarguable success in marking the entry of China's high-speed rail technology and equipment into Turkey, a country whose entry threshold is higher as it adopts European technology standards. This first success will no doubt create favorable conditions for China to enter other European railway markets.

China's technology and experience in rail construction has clearly gained recognition from Brazilian authorities. The president of Brazil, Dilma Rousseff, has repeatedly stated that Brazil hopes China can provide more help in building Brazil's railway network. Though Brazil is a great emerging economic power, there are myriad bottlenecks and lacunae in its infrastructure construction capacity, especially in its rail technology. China, on the other hand, has unmatched technology, excellent construction ability, and a wealth of experience in railroad construction. And Chinese enterprises also have a strong desire to cooperate with Brazil. There can be no doubt that prospects are bright for cooperation between China and Brazil in railroad construction.

The Mombasa-Nairobi high-speed railway is a critical infrastructure project to boost regional trade and deepen integration in East Africa. It is also the first new railway for 100 years in Kenya. It is totally contracted to and organized by Chinese enterprises, and is the first project that fully adopts Chinese standards. Once it is complete, transport times along the route will be halved, driving local economic development and acting as the catalyst for a broader program of investment. It is sure to be a milestone in the history of Kenya's economic development.

Questions:

(1) What are the advantages of China's high-speed railway when exploiting the overseas market?

(2) Where will be the major overseas market for China's high-speed railway?

(3) How does the construction of China's high-speed railway affect the trade between China and the other country?

(4) What do you think of the globalization of China's high-speed railway?
(Source: People's Daily Overseas Edition, author: Ding Xiaoxi, Wang Zicheng, Li Ming, Zheng Jinfa, Chen Weihua, Zhao Yan.)

V. Please complete the B/L with the given information.

Additional Information

（1）品名描述：P. P INJECTION CASES, ZL0322+BC05 230 SETS, ZL0319+BC01 230SETS DETALS AS PER SALES CONTRACT GW2005M06 DATED APR 22ND, 2005 CIF HESINKI, L/C NO. LRT9802457, DATE. APR 28TH, 2005.

CY/CY CONTAINER NO. 123

ZL0322+BC05

ZL0319+BC01

（2）买方：F. T. C. CO. AKEKSANTERINK AUTO P. O. BOX 9, FINLAND

（3）卖方：GREAT WALL TRADING CO., LTD. RM201, HUASHENG BUILDING, NINGBO, P. R CHINA

（4）收货人：TO ORDER

（5）装运港：NINGBO

（6）卸货港：HELSINKI

（7）船名船次：YANGFNA V.009W

（8）毛重：ZL0322+BC05   4255KGS
　　　　　ZL0319+BC01   4255KGS

（9）体积：ZL0322+BC05   34M3
　　　　　ZL0319+BC01   34M3

（10）提单号：CSC020867

（11）填单原件：3 SETS

BILL OF LADING

1. Shipper Insert Name, Address and Phone	B/L No.
(2)	(1)

2. Consignee Insert Name, Address and Phone

(3)

中远集装箱运输有限公司

COSCO CONTAINER LINES
TLX: 33057 COSCO CN
FAX: +86(021) 65458984
ORIGINAL
Port-to-Port or Combined Transport

3. Notify Party Insert Name, Address and Phone
(It is agreed that no responsibility shall be attached to the Carrier or his agents for failure to notify)

(4)

BILL OF LADING

4. Combined Transport* Pre-carriage by	5. Combined Transport* Place of Receipt	RECEIVED in external apparent good order and condition except as other-wise noted. The total number of packages or unites stuffed in the container, the description of the goods and the weights shown in this Bill of Lading are furnished by the Merchants, and which the carrier has no reasonable means of checking and is not a part of this Bill of Lading contract. The carrier has issued the number of Bills of Lading stated below, all of this tenor and date, one of the original Bills of Lading must be surrendered and endorsed or signed against the delivery of the shipment and whereupon any other original Bills of Lading shall be void. The Merchants agree to be bound by the terms and conditions of this Bill of Lading as if each had personally signed this Bill of Lading. SEE clause 4 on the back of this Bill of Lading (Terms continued on the back hereof, please read carefully). *Applicable Only When Document Used as a Combined Transport Bill of Lading.
6. Ocean Vessel Voy. No. (11)	7. Port of Loading (5)	
8. Port of Discharge	9. Combined Transport* Place of Delivery (6)	

Marks & Nos. Container/Seal No.	No. of Containers or Packages	Description of Goods (If Dangerous Goods, See Clause 20)	Gross Weight Kgs	Measurement
ROYAL 05AR225031 JEDDAH C/N: 1-UP	CBHU 0611758/ 25783 CY/CY PACKED IN 460CTNS	(7)	(8)	(9)
TOTAL	460CTNS	FREIGHT PREPAID	8510KGS	68M3
		Description of Contents for Shipper's Use Only (Not part of This B/L Contract)		

10. Total Number of containers and/or packages (in words)

Subject to Clause 7 Limitation

11. Freight & Charges Declared Value Charge	Revenue Tons	Rate	Per	Prepaid **Yes**	Collect
Ex. Rate:	Prepaid at **CHINA**	Payable at		Place and date of issue **MAY25th,2005.NINGBO,P.RCHINA.**	
	Total Prepaid	No. of Original B(s)/L (10)		Signed for the Carrier, COSCO CONTAINER LINES **ANDYLVKING**	

LADEN ON BOARD THE VESSEL
DATE
MAY 25, 2005 BY COSCO CONTAINER
LINES ENDORSED IN BLANK ON THE BACK

(1) _____
(2) _____
(3) _____
(4) _____
(5) _____
(6) _____
(7) _____
(8) _____
(9) _____
(10) _____
(11) _____

VI. Please finish the writing task for a shipping notice. Have a peer review and check who has done better.

Chapter 8 Insurance

Task Driven

South Africa Sprout International Corporation and Fujian Mushroom Import & Export Co., Ltd. agreed to trade based on CIF price terms. The seller will insure the buyer against All Risks, but the buyer requests to add war risk and agrees that the additional premium will be at their own expense. Please work in groups to write a confirmation email for the insurance purchase on behalf of the seller (Fujian Mushroom Import & Export Co., Ltd.).

Learning Objectives

• **Knowledge objectives:** Understanding the concept of insurance and marine cargo insurance; Be familiar with various risks covered under an insurance policy.
• **Skill objectives:** Draft an insurance email; Check insurance policies.
• **Affective objectives:** Improve self-protection and safety awareness.

Core Concept

 ## Insurance and Marine Cargo Insurance

Insurance is the practice of sharing among many persons risks of life or property that would otherwise be suffered by only a few.

By contrast, marine cargo insurance indicates that the insurant enters with an insurance company and/or an underwriter into a contract of insurance in which the insurance company will, according to the terms indicated in the insurance contract, indemnify the insurant of any loss that occurs within the scope of coverage.

An insurance policy is a contract of insurance, for which one party agrees to accept the risk (the insurer) and the other party seeks protection from the risks (the insured). In return for payment of a premium, the insurer will pay the insured a stated sum if event covered against occurs. The premium is paid by the insured, considered as a percentage of the sum insured.

8.2 Risks

The PICC has its own insurance clauses, known as China Insurance Clauses (CIC), which is different from the Institute Cargo Clauses (ICC). Based on the Ocean Marine Cargo Clauses of PICC, we usually have the following risks:

(1) Free from Particular Average (F.P.A.);

(2) With Average (W.A.) or With Particular Average (W.P.A);

(3) All Risks (A.R.).

FPA includes the total actual loss and constructive loss due to natural calamities and total and partial loss due to accidents.

W.P.A has a wider coverage than FPA. It provides extensive cover against all loss or damage due to marine perils throughout the duration of the policy, including partial losses of the insured goods due to natural calamities like heavy weather, lightning, tsunami, and earthquake.

A.R. is the most comprehensive risk, under which the insurer is responsible for all, total or partial loss of or damage of the goods insured either from sea perils or general external risks including the following general additional risks:

(1) Theft Pilferage and Non-Delivery, T.P.N.D.;

(2) Fresh Water Rain Damage, F.W.R.D.;

(3) Risk of Shortage;

(4) Risk of Intermixture and Contamination;

(5) Risk of Leakage;

(6) Risk of Clash and Breakage;

(7) Risk of Ordour;

(8) Damage Caused by Sweating and Heating;

(9) Hook Damage;

(10) Risk of Rust.

Apart from the above general risks, some special additional risks are also provided against the loss of or damage to the goods, which is not covered in A.R.:

(1) War Risks;

(2) Strike Risks;

(3) Aflatoxin;

(4) Failure to deliver;

(5) On Deck;

(6) Import Duty;
(7) Rejection.

8.3 A Letter for Discussing the Details of Coverage

Dear Sir,

We thank you for your letter of 27th March regarding the coverage, and the relevant details as follows:

(1) All Risks: Generally, we cover insurance W.P.A. and War Risk in the absence of definite instructions from our clients. If you want to insure against All Risks, we can provide such coverage at a slightly higher premium;

(2) Breakage: Breakage is a special risk, for which an extra premium will have to be charged. The present rate is about 0.7%. Claims are payable only for that part of the loss that is over 5%;

(3) Value to be insured: We note that you wish us to insure shipments to you for 10% above the invoice value, which is having our due attention.

We trust the above information will be helpful and await your further news.

Yours sincerely,
Jenny

8.4 A Letter for Informing the Arrangement of Insurance

Hi, Jenny

We have received your letter dated 29th May, requesting us to effect insurance on the captioned shipment for your account.

We are pleased to inform you that we have covered the above shipment with the People's Insurance Company of China against All Risks for $2,300. The policy is being prepared accordingly and will be sent to you by the end of this week together with our debit note for the premium.

For your information, we are making arrangements to ship the 350 cases of toys by S/S Hefeng, sailing on or about 15th of July.

Best,
Smith

Note:

(1) effect insurance on the captioned shipment (就标题商品投保)

Similar expressions include:

① arrange insurance on the goods against… risks

② to provide insurance…

③ to take out insurance⋯
④ to cover insurance⋯
(2) for your account (由你方承担费用)
Similar expressions include:
① to be borne by
② to be responsible for

Language Points

Words and Expressions

the insurant/insured/assured	投保人
the insurer/underwriter	保险公司
the claimant	索赔人
debit note	借款通知书
insurance policy	保险单
insurance certificate	保单凭证
insurance coverage	保险范围
insurance premium	保险费
premium rebate	保险费回扣
premium tariff	保险费率表
extra premium	额外保险费
insurance amount	保险金额
insurance broker	保险经纪人
insurance agent	保险代理商
perils of the sea	海上风险
natural calamities	自然灾害
fortuitous accidents	意外事故
External Risks	外来风险
General Additional Risks	一般外来风险
Special Additional Risks	特殊外来风险
Average	海损
Total Loss	全损
Actual Total Loss	实际全损
Constructive Total Loss	推定全损
Partial Loss	部分损失
General Average	共同海损
Particular Average	单独海损
sue and labor expenses	施救费用
salvage charges	救助费用

Theft Pilferage and Non-Delivery, T.P.N.D.	偷窃、提货不到险
Fresh Water Rain Damage, F.W.R.D.	淡水雨淋险
Risk of Shortage	短量险
Risk of Intermixture and Contamination	混杂、玷污险
Risk of Leakage	渗漏险
Risk of Clash and Breakage	碰损、破碎险
Risk of Ordour	串味险
Damage Caused by Sweating and Heating	受潮受热险
Hook Damage	钩损险
Loss and Damage Caused by Breakage of Packing	包装破裂险
Risk of Rust	锈损险
War Risks	战争险
Strike Risks	罢工险
Aflatoxin	黄曲霉素险
Failure to Deliver	交货不到险
On Deck	舱面险
Import Duty	进口关税险
Rejection	拒收险

Sentences

1. The cover shall be limited to sixty days upon discharge of the insured goods from the seagoing vessel at the final port of discharge.

被保险货物在卸货港卸离海轮后,保险责任以60天为限。

2. We generally insure W.P.A. on CIF sales.

按到岸价交易,我们一般保水渍险。

3. The additional premium is for the buyer's account.

增加的费用由买方负担。

4. We cover insurance on the 100 tons of wool.

我方为这100吨羊毛办理保险。

5. We cannot comply with your request for insuring your order for 130% of its invoice value.

我方不能为你方订货办理按发票金额130%的保险。

6. This kind of additional risk is coverable at 2%.

这种附加险的保险费是2%。

7. This risk is coverable at a premium of 5%.

这类保险按照5%的保险费投保。

8. Insurance on the goods shall be covered by us for 110% of the CIF value, and any extra premium for additional coverage, if required, shall be borne by the buyer.

将由我方按照到岸价的发票金额110%办理该货的保险,如果需要,额外增加保险的费用将由买方承担。

9. We would like to cover our ordered goods against W.P.A. for 120% of the invoice

value according to our usual practice.

我们要求根据实际对我们订购的货物按发票金额120%投保水渍险。

10. There are not delicate goods that can be damaged on the voyage. FPA will be good enough.

航行中不是精致的货物不易受损，所以平安险就足够了。

11. I'm afraid that W.P.A. coverage is too narrow for a shipment of this nature. Please extend the coverage to include T.P.N.D..

恐怕这种运输条件仅有水渍险范围太窄，请另加盗窃和提货不着险。

12. Would you insure our goods to be shipped from Shanghai to Lisbon next month?

你方对我方下月从上海到里斯本的货物投保了吗？

13. We should be glad if you would provide an insurance coverage of $390,000 on computers in transit from Tokyo to Beijing.

如果你方能提供我们从东京到北京的计算机39万美金的保险，我们将非常感谢。

14. Please insure us against All Risks of $300,000 value for 5,000 sets of "Butterfly" sewing machines sailing for New York.

请给我方到纽约的5000套"蝴蝶"牌缝纫机按30万美金投保一切险。

15. Please insure for me against all risks for 200 pieces of high-quality furniture valued at $20,000.

请为我方就200套高质量家具按2万美金投一切险。

16. We shall shortly be making regular shipments of leather goods to Canada, and shall be glad if you will issue an All Risks marine insurance policy for $70,000 to cover these shipments.

若为我方不久出口到加拿大的皮革品按7万美金投保海运一切险，我方将不胜感激。

17. I have some glassware to be shipped to Hong Kong. What risks should I cover?

我方有货要运到香港，我要保什么险？

18. Please let us know the premium of breakage.

请告诉我们破损险的保险费。

19. If we insure against free particular average, can you compensate us for all the losses if the ship sinks or bums, or gets stuck?

如果我们投保平安险，在船只沉没、遗失或角礁情况下贵方能否赔偿我们所有损失？

20. We have arranged insurance on your consignment of electric motor cars to be shipped in these ten days.

我们已为你们10日内发出的电动汽车货物投保。

21. We may cover the inland insurance on your behalf, but you will pay the additional premium.

我们可为贵方利益考虑投保内地险，但保险费应由贵司承担。

22. We shall insure the goods on your behalf.

为贵司利益着想，我们将为这批货投保。

23. Please give us the policy rates for FPA coverage and for W.P.A. coverage.

请给我们关于平安险和水渍险的投保率方案。

24. I would like to get an AR insurance policy. That way, we will be covered for any kind

of loss or damage.

我想获得一切险保险条例，也就是说保险要涵盖各种丢失或损失。

E-mail 1: from the buyer to seller

Hi Jenny,

As we need insurance for this shipment, would you apply for that as soon as possible?

Please kindly make a confirmation.

Best regards,

David

E-mail 2: from the seller to buyer

Hi David,

As the price we quoted to you is based on CIF, please kindly check the attached insurance draft and confirm if everything is correct. The insurance premium will be borne by us.

Thanks.

Jenny

E-mail 3: from the buyer to seller

Hi Jenny,

All the information on insurance draft is correct. Please process.

Kindly send us the original hard copy by DHL with other sea shipping documents.

Thanks.

David

E-mail 4: from the seller to buyer

Hi David,

Thanks for your final confirmation. We will send you the final hardcopy insurance as well as other shipping documents by DHL soon .

Have a nice day.

Jenny

Case Analysis

Business practice

In international trade, goods are subject to damage or loss because of various risks in the course of transit, loading and unloading. It is necessary for the buyer or the seller to arrange insurance before shipment. Emails concerned with insurance usually involve such topics as insured value, premium, risks and coverage. In this case, the deal was concluded on CIF basis, so the general practice was for the seller to cover the insurance and bear the relevant expenses. Therefore, David urged Jenny to buy the insurance as soon as possible. In response, Jenny agreed to the request, and purchased the insurance on her own. After the insurance draft was drawn up, Jenny sent him the policy for his confirmation. With the buyer's acceptance, she would forward the original insurance policy to the buyer, together with other shipping documents. These shipping documents can be used for taking delivery of goods and filing a claim with the insurance company in the case of cargo loss during transit.

Writing strategy

The emails are organized as follows:

(1) To request the seller to cover insurance on behalf of the buyer;

(2) To specify such information as the amount insured, coverage and premium, and send insurance draft for the seller's confirmation;

(3) To send the buyer the original insurance policy after it is finalized.

Business terms

(1) insurance premium: Insurance premium is a payment made to an insurance company in return for which the company agrees to pay for loss, as damages or expenses for goods insured, usually up to a particular amount.

(2) DHL: DHL is part of the world's leading postal and logistics company Deutsche Post DHL Group. It connects people in over 220 countries and territories worldwide. DHL engages in pick up and delivery services for parcels, documents and lightweight goods. DHL provides the following services: international express deliveries; global freight forwarding by air, sea,

road and rail; warehousing solutions from packaging to repairs and storage; mail deliveries worldwide; and other customized logistic services.

I. Choose the best answer.

1. A contract of insurance is established in the form of _____.
   A. policy   B. confirmation   C. order   D. offer
2. In order to cover certain risks, the insured must pay the_____.
   A. insured amount B. premium   C. price   D. shipping space
3. Which of the following is a Principle Risk?
   A. T.P.N.D.   B. Risk of Shortage C. War Risk   D. All Risks
4. Which of the following is Special Additional Risk?
   A. Leaking Risk   B. Hook Damage Risk
   C. Strike Risk   D. Taint of Odor Risk
5. Which of the following risks would you most likely cover for shipment of grain?
   A. Risk of Clash and Breakage   B. Leakage Risk
   C. Aflatoxin Risk   D. War Risk
6. Under which of the following price terms will the seller arrange for insurance?
   A. FOB   B. CFR   C. CIF   D. FAS
7. All Risks include_____.
   A. Special Additional Risks   B. General Additional Risks
   C. On Deck Risk   D. Rejection Risk
8. Since three-fifths of the voyage is in tropical weather and the goods are liable to go moldy, we think it is advisable to have the shipment_____the risk of mould.
   A. covered insurance   B. taken out insured
   C. covered against   D. insured for
9. If you_____insured against All Risks, we can comply with your request.
   A. wish that the goods would be   B. hope the goods to be
   C. request the goods to be   D. hope to have the goods
10. Please arrange_____our order for 130% of the invoice value.
   A. insurance on   B. cover at
   C. insurance cover in   D. risk

II. Translation.

Part One

Direction: Translate the following sentences into Chinese.

1. Insurance is to be effected by us for 110% of the invoice value against All Risks based on warehouse to warehouse clauses.

2. According to your instruction, we covered insurance against W.P.A. and T.P.N.D. for the consignments.

3. We regret to find that in addition to W.P.A., you require insurance to cover T.P.N.D. and SRCC which were not agreed upon by both parties during our negotiations.

4. We accept the quotation of insurance premium of 5% by the People's Insurance Company of China, and request you for arrangement to cover insurance F.P.A. on the delivery of 400 ton fertilizer to Bombay, India.

5. We usually insure the goods sold on CIF basis with our underwriter, The People's Insurance Company of China (PICC) for 110% of the total invoice value against All Risks and War Risk as per the Ocean Marine Cargo Clauses of the PICC of January 1st, 1981.

Part Two

Direction: Translate the following sentences into English.

6. 我们按发票金额的110%，为100公吨①羊毛投保了一切险。
7. 在没有客户明确指示的情况下，我们通常会投保水渍险和战争险。
8. 如果需要扩大保险范围，额外的保费将由你方支付。
9. 在运输过程中可能发生此类损坏，因此我们必须为货物投保以防破损风险。
10. 为了节省时间并简化程序，我们现在希望贵方能办理货物的投保。

III. Complete the sentences with the appropriate words given below.

cover	covered	covers	covering
coverage	insure	insurance	effected

1. Please_____against All Risks.
2. This insurance policy_____us against T.P.N.D..
3. We will_____W.P.A. insurance.
4. The documents will be sent to you under separate_____.
5. We have to point out that our letter of March 11st has fully_____this matter.
6. We send you herewith a copy of B/L_____shipment of 50 metric tons of Walnuts.
7. We have pleasure in advising shipment of your Order No.2354_____50 metric tons of Small Red Beans.
8. Insurance on the goods shall be_____by us for 110% of the CIF value.
9. We shall provide such_____at your cost.
10. Insurance is to be_____by the buyers under FOB terms.

IV. Extensive reading.

Cooperative Principle

Paul Grice, a famous American philosopher, proposed a theory of conversation which consists

---

① 1公吨=1吨。国际贸易中常用单位为公吨。

of a Cooperative Priciple (CP) in the article "Logic and Conversation" in 1975. The principle is based on the assumption that participants in a conversation cooperate with each other and usually attempt to be truthful, informative, relevant, and clear in order to facilitate successful communication. It is composed of four conversational maxims as follows.

The maxim of quantity:

It requires the speaker to provide necessary information and not to offer redundant information.

a. Make your contribution as informative as is required.

b. Do not make your contribution more informative than that is required.

c. The violation of quantity maxim: It means the speaker does not provide enough information or give more or less information than its actual need in a conversation.

The maxim of quality

It requires the speaker to make your contribution one that is true.

a. Do not say what you believe to be false.

b. Do not say that for which you lack adequate evidence.

c. The violation of quality maxim: It refers to offering false messages deliberately or saying something which do not have enough evidence.

The maxim of relevance

It requires the speaker to say related words, and raised questions by the speaker can not be avoided or irrelevantly answered.This maxim also helps us to understand utterances in conversations that may not be initially obvious.

The maxim of manner

It refers to the choice of words you use. For example, we should avoid using big or overly complex words we know our listener will not understand, and we should try our best to be concise and coherent.

a. Avoid obscurity or ambiguity;

b. Be brief;

c. Be orderly.

Please complete the following tasks.

Task 1. Questions:

(1) What is the cooperative principle?

(2) What maxims does the cooperative principle have?

Task 2. Group Work

What kinds of cooperative principle maxims do the dialogue violate? Can you complete the dialogue in a better way according to the cooperative maxims?

(1) A: Where does Jack live?   B: Somewhere in China.

(2) A: Can you tell me the time?   B: Well, the milkman has come.

(3) A: I like dogs, there are 3 dogs in my home.

　　B: That is because you are an adult. Every child fears dogs.

(4) A: What did you do last night?

　　B: I reviewed my lessons and finished my homework, because I will hang out with my friends today and we will play tennis this afternoon.

(5) A: What are you going to do after school?

　　B: I'm going home to make dinner and sleep.

V. Please fill in the Insurance Policy with the given information.

A. L/C information

Applicant	*50:	ZELLERS INC. , ATTN. IMPORT DEPT.		
		401 BAY STREET, 10/FL.		
		TORONTO ON MJH. 2Y4, CANADA		
Beneficiary	*59:	G.M.G. HARDWEAR & TOOLS IMP. & EXP.		
		COMPANY LTD.		
		726 DONGFENG ROAD EAST, GUANGZHOU, CHINA		
Loading in Charge	44A:	GUANG ZHOU, CHINA		
For Transport to…	44B:	VANCOUVER, CANADA		
Descript. of Goods	45A:	HANDLE TOOLS		
		ITEM NO.	QUANTITY	UNTI PRICE
		A 0214	2,000 DOZ	USD 10.50
		A 0012	1,000 DOZ	USD 11.50
		M 0102	500 DOZ	USD 28.00
		AS PER SALES CONFIRMATION NO. 02GP520471		
		DD 03 JAN.02		
		CIF VANCOUVER CANADA		
Documents Required	46A:	+ MARINE INSURANCE POLICY OR CERTIFICATE IN DUPLICATE, ENDORSED IN BLANK, FOR FULL INVOICE VALUE PLUS 10 PERCENT, STATING CLAIM PAYABLE IN CANADA COVERING INSTITUTE CARGO CLAUSES(A) AND WAR RISKS.		

B. Other information

Invoice No.: KW-030419

Date of Invoice: 2018 年 4 月 10 日

Amount: USD46,500.00

Date of B/L: 2018 年 4 月 19 日

Vessel Name: CHAOHE/ZIM CANADA V. 44E WITH TRANSHIPMENT AT HK

Shipping Mark: ZELLERS CANADA/VANCOUVER

Insurance Policy No.: KC03-85362

Packing: 10DOZ/PACKACE 350PACKACES

中国人民保险公司
The People's Insurance Company of China
总公司设于北京 1949 年创立
Head Office Beijing Established in 1949

Invoice No. __(1)__   Policy No. __(2)__

海洋货物运输保险单
MARINE CARGO TRANSPORTATION INSURANCE POLICY

被保险人：_____
Insured：__(3)__

中保财产保险有限公司（以下简称本公司）根据被保险人的要求，及其所缴付约定的保险费，按照本保险单承担险别和背面所载条款与下列特别条款承保下列货物运输一切险和战争险，特签发本保险单。

This policy of Insurance witnesses that the People's Insurance (Property) Company of China, Ltd. (hereinafter called "the Company"), the request of the Insured and in consideration of the agreed premium paid by the Insured, undertakes to insure the undermentioned goods against All Risk and War Risk in transportation subject to the condition of the Policy as per the Clauses printed overleaf and other special clauses attached hereon.

保险货物项目 Description of Goods	包装 单位 数量 Packing Unit Quantity	保险金额 Amount Insured
(4)	(5)	(6)

承保险别   货物标记 __(7)__
Condition   Marks of Goods

COVERING INSTITUTE CARGO CLAUSES(A) AND WAR RISKS

总保险金额： (8)
The Amount Insured:

保费   载运输工具   开航日期
Premium as Arranged   Per Conveyance S.S. (9)   Sig. on or abt. (10)

起运港   目的港
From GUANGZHOU   To VANCOUVER W/T HONGKONG

所保货物，如发生本保险单项下可能引起索赔的损失或损坏，应立即通知本公司下述代理人查勘。如有索赔，应向本公司提交保险单正本（本保险单共有 1 份正本）。及有关文件。如一份正本已用于索赔，其余正本则自动失效。

In the event of loss or damage which may result in a claim under this Policy, immediate notice must be given to the Company's Agent as mentioned hereunder. Claims, if any, one of the Original Policy which has been issued in ONE Original(s) together with the relevant documents shall be surrendered to the Company. If one of the Original Policy has been accomplished, the others to be void.

中保财产保险有限公司
THE PEOPLE'S INSURANCE (PROPERTY) COMPANY OF CHINA, LTD

(1) _____
(2) _____
(3) _____
(4) _____
(5) _____
(6) _____
(7) _____
(8) _____
(9) _____
(10) _____

VI. Writing practice.

Please finish a confirmation email for the insurance purchase on behalf of the seller based on the writing task. Afterwards, you can have a peer review to assess the result.

Chapter 9 Claim and Settlement

Task Driven

After receiving the goods, South Africa Sprout International Corporation found that 2 boxes of the goods were damaged in their packaging and the goods had some degree of moisture, so they filed a claim for a 20% price reduction. Students are required to lodge a claim on behalf of the buyer. Please analyze the reasons and draft a claim email.

Learning Objectives

• **Knowledge objectives:** Tell the difference between claim and complaint; Recite useful expressions for claim and settlement.
• **Skill objectives:** Master the procedure and the skills of lodging a claim properly; Draft a letter of complaint or claim in a polite way.
• **Affective objectives:** Develop professional ethics; Keep harmonious relationships with others.

Core Concept

9.1 Claim and Settlement

A claim means that in international trade, if one party breaches the contract and causes losses to the other party directly or indirectly, the party suffering losses may make a complaint or lodge a claim.

When complaint occurs regarding the delivery, quality, weight, package, etc., the buyer will ask the seller to make compensations and settle the problem. The seller will investigate the matter and settle the problem in a satisfactory way.

Usually, it is the buyer who will make a complaint. However, sometimes even the seller can do it due to some reasons, such as a breach of the contract or late establishment of L/C. In the contract, two parties often stipulate clauses on settlement of a claim as well as inspection and claim clauses.

9.2 Factors Leading to a Claim

It is common that claims take place in international trade. A claim happens when the goods delivered by the seller is not in accordance with the contracted quantity, quality, specifications; when the seller fails to make timely delivery or refuses to make delivery; and when the goods are damaged due to improper packing or in transit. In brief, a claim may occur where poor quality, late shipment, shortage, wrong articles, damage, or being wrongly billed turn up.

9.3 Contents of Lodging a Claim

9.3.1 Claim Proof

In order to persuade the other party to acknowledge your claim, you should provide some necessary documents as proofs, such as original insurance policy, commercial invoice, packing list, B/L, survey report, or certificate of loss or damage. Generally, relevant proofs and issuing institution are included in claim clauses.

9.3.2 Claim Period

It is required that the period of a claim should be stipulated in the contract when the claiming party hopes to defend his interests. The claimed party can deny the other party for the claim when the period it expires.

9.3.3 Claim Amount

Claim amount includes the invoice value of a contract and incidental damages such as inspection fees, loading and unloading expenses, bank charges, storage charges and interest, etc..

9.3.4 Claim Requirement

There are some reasons leading to a claim or complaint, including poor quality, late shipment, shortage of goods, wrong goods or damage of goods. These reasons will lead to the importer to make various claim requirements, such as asking for a discount, replenishment, replacement, repair, return and refund.

9.3.4 Claim Principles

While lodging your claim, please come up with a clear proposition and state your claim politely and firmly. Your claim letter should include referring to the last letter, identifying the situation, stating your reasons, making a requirement or suggestion, and ending the letter politely.

9.4 Settlement of a Claim

Usually, we should deal with a claim promptly and properly. That is to say, first we should analyze and investigate the case carefully and figure out who will take the responsibility. Then we can inform the other party of the response in time. Normally, there are two ways of response. One is to accept, settle or entertain a claim. The other is to reject, withdraw or waive a claim.

In order to cope with a claim, an adjustment letter is quite necessary. We can classify the adjustment letter into 3 types: full adjustment, partial adjustment, and refusal. Full adjustment means that you grant the claim completely. Partial adjustment indicates that you grant the claim partially and suggest them to refer to a third party for compensation, such as the insurance company or carrier, etc. Refusal means that you reject the claim if it is unfounded or unjustifiable.

9.5 Sample Letters for Claim and Settlement

Sample One

Sub: Order No. DL201
Date: 13rd October 2021
Dear Lucy,
    We have received the 500 cases of electric toys under the Order No. DL201 you shipped per S.S. "Peace". But much to our regret, after carefully examination, we are

disappointed at their inferior quality. They certainly do not match the sample you sent us. Some of them are so poor that we can not help feel there must have been some mistakes in making up the order.

As the materials are quite unsuited to the needs of our customers and we have no choice but to ask you to take them back and return the invoice value and the inspection charges involved, with the total of US $900. Enclosed please find our Survey Report No. 341.

We trust you will settle this claim promptly to safeguard the goodwill of your company.

Sincerely,
Smith

Sample Two

Sub: Claim on Order No. DL201
Date: 14th October 2021
Dear Smith,

We have just received your email of October 13rd together with a copy of Survey Report No. 341 and have given it our prompt attention. We wish to express our deepest regret over the unfortunate incident. You must have had much difficulty in meeting the orders of your clients.

After a check-up by our staff in Shanghai, we found that the workers did the wrong package by putting the goods of Order No.DL200 into the case of your Order No. DL201, thus resulting in the mismatch of the products. This was due to the negligence of our employees, for which we tender our apologies.

Accordingly, we will deliver the right order to you through the earliest vessel this month and compensate you at the value of US $200 for the loss you have suffered. We promise this kind of accident will never occur and you will receive an extra discount on your next order.

We hope that the arrangement we have made will satisfy you.

Best,
Lucy

Words and Expressions

claims	索赔
forwarder	运输商
settlement of claim	理赔
refund	归还，偿还

the parties concerned	合同当事人
contingency	意外事故
break the contract	违约
dented	碰凹
suffer losses	受损
crushed	压碎
compensation	赔偿
mildew	发霉
carrier	承运人
tainted	污染
claim clauses	索赔条款
cracked	破裂
proofs	索赔依据
spotty	有污点
period for claim	索赔时限
conglomeration	结块
claim amount	索赔金额
water stain	水渍
penalty	罚金
vermin bitten	虫咬
irretrievably	不可挽回地
arbitration	仲裁
short-delivered/landed	短交
settle	解决，清偿
claim for	表示索赔原因，索赔的金额
claim on	表示对某批货物索赔
claim against	表示向某人、某公司索赔
file/make/lodge/raise/enter/register a claim against sth.	就…提出
accept a claim	同意索赔
entertain a claim	受理索赔
reject a claim	拒绝索赔
settle a claim	解决索赔
waive a claim	放弃索赔
withdraw a claim	撤回索赔
complain to sb. of /about sth.	因某事而向某人抱怨
settlement of disputes	解决争端
settle a claim	理赔
settlement options	索赔选择权
arbitration clause	仲裁条款
arbitration award	仲裁裁决

arbitration application	仲裁申请
arbitration procedure	仲裁程序
arbitrator	仲裁员，仲裁人
match the sample	与样品相符
compensate partly	部分赔偿
resort to litigation	打官司
withhold business	停止交易
in/under dispute	在争议中的
compensate for sth.	赔偿
the claiming party	索赔方
the claimed party	理赔方

Sentences

1. We are sorry to inform you that the goods forwarded to us are not up to the standards demanded.
非常遗憾地通知你方，发运给我方的货物没有达到规定的标准。

2. We very much regret that the folded chairs supplied by you under Order No. 225 have not yet reached us up to now.
我方深感遗憾你方按我方第225号订单供应的折叠椅至今尚未到货。

3. Claim is filed for the shortage of kids shoes shipped on board S.S. "Great Wall" which arrived here on May 4th.
"长城"货轮于5月4日抵达本港。我方发现所运童鞋数量短缺，特向贵方提出索赔。

4. We have to lodge a claim against you for a short delivery of 500kg.
由于贵方发货短缺500千克，因此我方提出索赔。

5. After inspecting your shipment of our order No.12, we found them short in weight by 1,500kg. Therefore, we raise a claim amounting to US $600 plus inspection charges.
经检验，贵方发给我方的第12号订单项下的货物短重1500千克，因此我们提出600美元的索赔，另加检验费。

6. Buyers have claimed on/upon us for short shipment.
买方已因短装向我方提出索赔。

7. We have already raised a claim against the insurance company for $500 for damage in transit.
货物因运输受损，我们已向保险公司提出要求赔偿500美元。

8. Our claim on your L/C No.100 has not been paid.
第100号信用证索汇尚未支付。

9. It is established beyond controversy that the shipping company is responsible for the damage of the goods in transit.
毫无疑问，船运公司对货物在运输途中受损负有责任。

10. After re-inspection, we found that the quality of the goods was not in conformity with the contract stipulations.

经复验，我方发现货物质量与合同规定不符。

11. After double-checking the goods against your invoice, we discovered a considerable shortage in number.

经复查发票，我方发现金额少了很多。

12. We claim $2,000 for short shipment on the 50 tons peanuts ex M.V. "Hongxing".

由"红星"轮运来的50吨花生，由于短装，我方提出索赔2000美元。

13. We request to extend the period for claim on the above shipment to the middle of April.

我方要求对上述货物的索赔时间期限延长至4月中旬。

14. Your claim should be supported by sufficient evidence.

贵方索赔须有充分的证据。

15. Our users insist that you have to compensate for the inferior quality.

我方用户坚持认为，贵方须为次质给予赔偿。

16. On the basis of the SIQA's Survey Report, we hereby register our claim with you as follows.

根据上海商品检验局的检验报告，特此向贵方提出如下索赔。

17. Survey Report No. SH(55)765 is herewith enclosed and we look forward to your settlement at an early date.

兹随附第SH（55）765号检验报告一份，盼贵方早日理赔。

18. We consider that the suppliers are responsible for the short weight, because 60 bags were found broken when unloading.

供应商须负短重责任，因为我方在卸货时发现60包破损。

19. The Survey Report certified that the quality of the above-mentioned goods is much inferior to that of the sample sent previously.

检验报告证明上述货物的品质与之前的样品相比差距很大。

20. We shall remit to you an amount of $600 in compensation for the loss you suffered from the incident.

现汇款600美元，以补偿因此事给贵方造成的损失。

21. Please be informed that the above mentioned goods will be, before the claim is settled, stored temporarily at the warehouse and insured on your behalf and the expenses of the storage and premium will be borne by you consequently.

在索赔了结之前，该货暂存于我方仓库并代为投保。所需仓储费用和保险费用日后向贵方收取。

22. As our shipping documents can confirm that the goods were in perfect condition when they left here, and that evidently shows they were damaged in transit. Therefore, we cannot give our consideration to your claim.

根据运输单据，货物离开此地时完好无损，这说明货物是在运输途中受损。据此，我方对贵方的索赔不予考虑。

23. We are taking the liberty of sending you an extra dozen of cotton pillowcases, at no cost, as a small compensation for your inconvenience.

我方冒昧寄去一打棉枕套，作为对贵方的一点补偿。

24. Should the responsibility of the subject under claim be found to rest on the part of our company, we shall send our reply to you together with suggestion for settlement within 20 days after receipt of your claim.

如属我方责任，我方会在收到贵方索赔 20 天内答复并提出处理意见。

25. The goods in question were in perfect conditions when they left our port as evidenced by the B/L.

该商品在离开我们港口时状况良好，有提单为证。

Case One

E-mail 1: from the buyer to seller

Dear Jenny,

We have got your goods. Thanks for the shipment. Upon checking, we found two boxes of items damp with packing damaged. Attached you will see the pictures and inspection report.

Therefore, we have to ask for a 20% deduction of the total amount of this contract as compensation.

Best regards,

David

Case One Analysis

Business practice

In fulfilling the order, sometimes the seller may receive complaints and claims raised by the buyer for various reasons, such as wrong delivery, short weight, delay of delivery, inferior quality and improper packing. However, not all the claims are justifiable, and some buyers may simply find fault with the goods as an excuse to cancel their contracts or ask for compensations. In this case, David found that some of the goods were damaged, and investigated the reasons for the packing damage. He sent Jenny photos and the inspection report to show the grounds for his claim. Meanwhile, he suggested the way compensations could be made.

Writing strategy

This email is organized as follows:

(1) To refer to the goods that have been received;

(2) To describe the problem or loss in detail;
(3) To present evidence such as a survey report or photos to support the claim;
(4) To suggest the ways to settle the problem and ask for compensations.

Pragmatic analysis

In this email, David filed a complaint and expressed his request in an appropriate manner. Firstly, he expressed thanks for receiving the goods instead of making the complaint immediately. Secondly, to support his claim, he presented evidence and referred to specific details, which showed a realistic attitude. For example, he provided accurate information and kept to the fact, by using expressions "two boxes of items damp" and "see the pictures and inspection report". Thirdly, he stated the request precisely and concisely. The requirement is expressed in concrete terms, as shown in the phrase "20% deduction of the total amount". Obviously, it is of great importance to communicate honestly and tactfully in writing emails to make a complaint.

Case Two

E-mail 2: from the seller to buyer

Dear David,

We are really sorry about this damage. As our shipping documents can confirm that the goods were in perfect condition when they left here, and that evidently shows they were damaged in transit. Therefore, we cannot give our consideration to your claim.

We have already raised a claim against the insurance company for $2,000 for the damage in transit. It is established beyond controversy that the shipping company is responsible for the damage of the goods in transit.

The insurance company will contact you to deal with this case. Hope it can be solved soon.

Best regards,

Jenny

Case Two Analysis

Business practice

On receiving a complaint, the seller should firstly make an investigation and determine whether the complaint is justifiable. If the complaint is reasonable, the seller needs to apologize immediately for the inconvenience and loss to the buyer and suggest a solution. However, if the complaint is groundless, the seller can choose to refuse adjustment of the claim. In this case, Jenny used the clean B/L as evidence to show that the goods were in order when they were loaded on board. To assist the buyer, Jenny also filed a complaint against the insurance company and shipping company, who might be held responsible for the loss. Although she did not agree with David's request for the compensation, she tried to help him solve this problem and showed her good will.

Writing strategy

This email is organized as follows:

(1) To show regret for the inconvenience or loss suffered by the buyer;

(2) To reject the claim and explain the reason for the problem on the ground of investigation;

(3) To suggest possible settlement options and provide necessary assistance;

(4) To express the hope that the issue can be solved.

Pragmatic analysis

In reply to emails of complaint, it is sometimes necessary to decline the customers' request for compensation and keep their good will in the meantime. In this case, Jenny tried to put herself in the customer's shoes, suggested an alternative, and helped out by raising a claim against the insurance company and shipping company. To make her emails more persuasive, she adopted the following pragmatic strategies. Firstly, she adopted the right tone, showing her regret and taking a firm position. She used expressions with the meaning of regret and assertiveness, such as "We are really sorry about" and "we cannot give our consideration to your claim". Secondly, she used shields to convey her attitude indirectly and add objectivity to the proposal, such as "As our shipping documents can confirm", "that evidently shows" and "It is established beyond controversy that", rather than using the first pronoun. These expressions provide the reason why she refused the customer's request for compensation. Thirdly, she included accurate facts, exact figures and action verbs so as to make her suggestion more concrete and convincing. She showed what she was doing to support the customer by using specific words such as "have already raised a claim", "$2,000" and "is responsible for". In this email, Jenny handled the complaint tactfully and amicably, which might be helpful in maintaining sound relationship with the customer.

I. Choose the best answer.

1. The goods were packed loose in the case_____sufficient padding_____causing the breakage of the articles.

    A. lacking, so   B. with, so   C. lack of, thus   D. without, thus

2. We believe that the cases were too _____ and the packing was not sufficient for sea transport.

A. weak　　　　B. big　　　　C. fragile　　　　D. huge

3. We found that 20 sets of recorders had _____ by sea-water, and seem to be a complete write-off.

A. been damaged　　B. damaged　　C. damaging　　D. been damaging

4. According to the contract stipulations, we are not _____ for the damage.

A. likely　　　　B. possible　　　　C. affordable　　　　D. liable

5. We regret that your claim could hardly be _____ as the goods were damaged _____ transit.

A. acceptable, in　　B. agreeable, as　　C. favorable, for　　D. capable, in

6. We regret that we cannot _____ your claim, which is without any foundation.

A. entrance　　　　B. entertain　　　　C. receive　　　　D. enter

7. We have _____ the drums one by one and found that most of them are leaking.

A. tested　　　　B. examined　　　　C. traced　　　　D. rolled

8. Twenty cases of Green Tea you sent us were found to be badly damaged. This was apparently attributable to _____ packing.

A. faulty　　　　B. domestic　　　　C. inferior　　　　D. outer

9. A few customers have complained _____ the packing of our export goods. Now we succeed _____ trying to put it right.

A. to, in　　　　B. about, in　　　　C. in, about　　　　D. in, to

10. Claims _____ shortage or incorrect material must be _____ within 30 days after arrival of the goods.

A. for, done　　　　B. done, for　　　　C. made, for　　　　D. for, made

II. Translation.

Part One

Direction: Translate the following sentences into Chinese.

1. Upon examining the goods, we discovered to our surprise that they were inferior in quality to the original samples.

2. We insist that you compensate the sum of our losses which were due to your improper packing.

3. In view of our long-standing business relations, we wish to settle the dispute in an amicable manner.

4. We regret to learn that 51 bags of rice were broken and seriously damaged by sea water. However, we are not the party to blame, therefore can not entertain your claim.

5. Your shipment of our order No.298 has been found short on weight by 1,000kg, for which we must file a claim amounting to $800 plus the inspection fee.

Part Two

Direction: Translate the following sentences into English.

6. 破损发生在运输过程中，应由航运公司负责。

7. 我方希望贵方能尽快解决索赔问题，并圆满结束此事。

8. 请尽快运送损坏货物的替代品，同时我们将向保险公司提出索赔。

9. 因你方未能及时发货而造成的所有损失，我方将提出索赔。

10. 我方将向贵公司汇出 620 美元，以赔偿贵方遭受的损失。

III. Fill in the blanks with appropriate words.

1. We are lodging_____the shipment ex s.s. "Red Star" _____ short delivery.

2. _____ examinations we found that the goods do not agree_____the original sample.

3. In_____of the long-standing business relations between us, we wish to meet half way to_____the claim.

4. We confirm_____received your remittance_____$879 in settlement of our claim.

5. Further to our fax of 26th November, we register a claim_____ $500 and enclose herewith a survey report_____by SCIB.

6. We hereby register our claim with you_____this cargo_____respect of quality.

7. We reserve the right to claim compensation_____you for any damage.

8. We apologize_____your trouble and promise to execute your future orders with maximum care and efficiency.

9. Should you not agree to accept our proposal, we would like to settle_____arbitration.

10. _____the basis of the Survey Report from the Commodity Inspection Bureau, we hereby register our claim with you.

11. It is estimated that there is a_____weight of 500kg in the shipment ex S.S. "Long Journey".

12. Insurance is to be_____by the buyer if a transaction is concluded on FOB or CFR basis.

13. We therefore wired you yesterday, requesting you to_____the insurance company directly.

14. We should be grateful if you would take the matter up for us_____the insurers.

IV. Extensive reading.

Winter Games All about Unity, Breaking Barriers

The ongoing Winter Paralympic Games, along with the Winter Olympics which concluded in February in 2022, grand sports events as they are, have facilitated cultural exchanges among countries.

The successful hosting of the 2022 Winter Olympics has neutralized Western efforts to vilify everything Chinese, by better telling its story to the world so as to help the international community better understand the truth about the country including its culture, history and contribution to the world.

Harmony is integral to Chinese culture, and China has always followed a policy of harmonious coexistence. That all things on the planet are interconnected is embedded in traditional Chinese culture. And as the opening ceremony of the Winter Games showed the ice hockey puck can break through the Water Cube and the five Olympic rings can break through the ice, meaning unnecessary barriers can be broken and conflicts resolved peacefully.

The opening ceremony also highlighted the importance of reducing carbon emissions and following the path of low-carbon development. The overall harmony and unity that the opening ceremony underlined, and the green development philosophy it emphasized characterize China's policies. These very factors have been behind the economic and social success of China, and it will continue to follow them.

Questions:

(1) Why have Winter Olympics facilitated cultural exchange?

(2) What is the relationship between harmony and Winter Olympics?

V. Group discussion.

Jennifer has received another complaint from her customer in Poland. Please read the following email and tell your teammates what is wrong with the goods. Can you use the theory of harmony to tackle this problem by providing a proper reply?

Hello Jennifer,

I got your goods, but unfortunately the quality of goods is drastically worse than your model we have from the fair and you have promised us!

The main points of our complaints after opening the 15 cartons are:

- There are many shoes with other logo than what we ordered.
- Logo is many times illegible and crookedly glued.
- On the side of shoes are a lot of fringes (not truncated endings).
- The shoes are in cartons crooked and suppressed.
- Colour navy is other than you showed us at the fair. The pictures with Adax seem like blue, not navy. Please see the below navy colour which I send you before for your confirmation.
- Sizes are not correct.

Only black shoes are correct!

All blue and navy are not correct and they are 2 sizes smaller. For example, the number 44 is 42, number 42 is 40 and so on!

Then we have big problems in contracting with our clients!

They refuse to take the worse goods and we do not earn the money but have to pay the penalty!

Separately I send you some photos of your goods and I'm waiting for your position! Could you please help me to do statistics first. Thanks in advance.

Regards,

Benjamin

VI. Writing practice.

Please finish the writing task about a claim email on behalf of South Africa Sprout International Corporation. Have a peer review to decide which one can adapt politeness principle and theory of harmony to solve this problem.

Bibliography

蔡惠伟，2012．外经贸函电教程[M].2 版．上海：华东理工大学出版社．
陈春媚，2016．外贸函电与单证实训教程[M].2 版．北京：对外经济贸易大学出版社．
陈拥宪，2015．外贸函电[M].上海：华东理工大学出版社．
甘鸿，1996．外经贸英语函电（英语读本）[M].Revised Edition．上海：上海科学技术文献出版社．
关彤，2010．社交礼仪[M].3 版．海口：南海出版社．
黄丽威，2006．外贸函电与单证[M].北京：高等教育出版社．
兰天，2015．外贸英语函电[M].7 版．大连：东北财经大学出版社．
李蓉，赵凤玉，2014．外贸函电与单证[M].北京：清华大学出版社，北京交通大学出版社．
李爽，2016．国际商务函电[M].2 版．北京：清华大学出版社．
李月菊，2010．国际贸易实务与操作（学生用书）[M].上海：上海外语教育出版社．
梁润森，2000，陈文明．新编经贸英语写作教程[M].北京：中国社会科学出版社．
刘刚，2015．进出口业务英语函电[M].北京：北京理工大学出版社．
戚云方，2012．新编外经贸英语函电与谈判[M].2 版．杭州：浙江大学出版社．
沈银珍，2010．会展英语[M].2 版．北京：中国人民大学出版社．
史兴松，2016．国际商务礼仪（英文版）[M].2 版．北京：对外经济贸易大学出版社．
隋思忠，2010．外贸英语函电[M].3 版．大连：东北财经大学出版社．
王虹，耿伟，2017．外贸英语函电[M].3 版．北京：清华大学出版社．
王晶，卓新光，孙凌，2014．商务英语函电[M].上海：外语教学与研究出版社．
王兴孙，张春锹，邬孝煜，2012．新编进出口英语函电[M].3 版．上海：外语教学与研究出版社．
王杏，2016．创业札记：金牌外贸业务员到 CEO 的华丽转身[M].广州：广东经济出版社．
王妍，刘亚卓，2011．外贸函电[M].2 版．北京：北京大学出版社．
冼燕华，余世明，陈梅，2016．新编国际商务英语函电[M].3 版．广州：暨南大学出版社．
杨晋，2011．当代国际商务函电[M].天津：天津大学出版社．
叶绍义，陈华，郭天宝，2012．创业管理：外贸企业视角[M].大连：东北财经大学出版社．
易露霞，刘洁，尤彧聪，2016．外贸英语函电[M].3 版．北京：清华大学出版社．
毅冰，2012．十天搞定外贸函电[M].北京：中国海关出版社．
毅冰，2012．外贸高手客户成交技巧[M].北京：中国海关出版社．
毅冰，2018．外贸高手客户成交技巧 2：揭秘买手思维[M].北京：中国海关出版社．
应颖，2015．国际商务礼仪基础[M].北京：高等教育出版社．
于晓云，2015．外贸函电[M].北京：首都经济贸易大学出版社．
余晓泓，董梅，孙瑞，2017．外贸英文函电[M].北京：清华大学出版社．
张爱玲，房爱群，2011．国际商务函电[M].北京：北京大学出版社．
张翠波，2013．实用商务英语信函写作[M].北京：清华大学出版社，北京交通大学出版社．

张真，刘玲玉，2016．国际商务礼仪（双语版）[M].北京：清华大学出版社．
赵银德，2010．外贸函电[M].2版．北京：机械工业出版社．
周瑞琪，王小鸥，徐月芳，2019．国际贸易实务（英文版）[M].4版．北京：对外经济贸易大学出版社．
曾勇民，2016．国际商务函电[M].2版．北京：北京理工大学出版社．

Appendix One

Letter of Credit

2001MAR22 09:18:11 日期 LOGICAL TERMINAL	E102 逻辑终端
MT S700	ISSUE OF A DOCUMENTARY CREDIT 开立跟单信用证
PAGE00001	FUNCMSG700
	UMR06881051

MSGACK DWS765I AUTH OK, KEY B198081689580FC5, BKCHCNBJ RJHISARI RECORO	
BASIC HEADER 基本报头（收电人代码）	F 01 BKCHCNBJA940 0588 550628
APPLICATION HEADER 应用报头（发电人代码）	0 700 1057 010320 RJHISARIAXXX 7277 977367 020213 1557 N *MITSUBISHI UFJ FINANCIAL GROUP, JAPAN *TOKYO *(HEAD OFFICE)开证行
USER HEADER 用户报头（终端行代码）	SERVICE CODE 103: (银行盖信用证通知专用章) BANK. PRIORITY 113: MSG USER REF. 108: INFO. FROM CI 115:
SEQUENCE OF TOTAL 页次	*27	1 / 1

SEQUENCE OF TOTAL 页次	*27	1 / 1
FORM OF DOC. CREDIT 信用证类别	*40A	IRREVOCABLE
DOC. CREDIT NUMBER 信用证号码	*20	0011LC123756
DATE OF ISSUE 开证日	31C	220320（2022 年 3 月 20 日）
DATE/PLACE EXP.（Expiry）到期日	*31D	DATE 220515 PLACE CHINA （2022 年 5 月 15 日中国到期）
APPLICANT 申请人	*50	SOUTH AFRICA SPROUT INTERNATIONAL CORP., JAPAN BRANCH TEL: 00813-1-4659220 FAX: 00813-1-4659213
BENEFICIARY 受益人	*59	FUJIAN XIANZHILOU NUTRA-INDUSTRY BLDG9, INNOVATION PARK, FUZHOU, HIGH-TECH ZONE, SHANGJIE, MINHOU, FUZHOU, FUJIAN, CHINA 350000
AMOUNT 信用证总额	*32B	CURRENCY USD AMOUNT 1,757, 800.00
AVAILABLE WITH/BY 押汇方式及地点	*41D	ANY (prime) BANK IN CHINA, BY NEGOTIATION（议付）
DRAFTS AT …汇票的种类、性质	42C	SIGHT（即期）
DRAWEE 汇票的受票人（付款人）	42A	RJHISARI *MITSUBISHI UFJ FINANCIAL GROUP, JAPAN TOKYO (HEAD OFFICE)
PARTIAL SHIPMTS 分装	43P	NOT ALLOWED
TRANSSHIPMENT 转运	43T	NOT ALLOWED
LOADING ON BRD/IN CHARGE 装运港	44A	CHINA MAIN DORT, CHINA
DESTINATION PORT 目的港 （FOR TRANSPORT TO 运往…）	44B	TOPYO PORT, JAPAN
LATEST SHIPMENT 装运期限	44C	220430（2022 年 4 月 30 日）

Continued

GOODS DESCRIPT. 货物描述	45A	ABOUT 1281 CARTONS GANODEMA SINENSE & GANODEMA LUCIDUM, 15731 KGS NET WEIGHT, 18935 KGS GROSS WEIGHT
DOCS REQUIRED 要求单证	46A	DOCUMENTS REQUIRED: DRAFTS ARE TO BE ACCOMPANIED BY THE FOLLOWING DOCUMENTS IN ENGLISH, IN DUPLICATE, UNLESS OTHERWISE SPECIFIED: 汇票必须与以下单证同时提供，除非另有规定，所有单证应提供2份，用英文制作。
一式三份签字的商业发票，发票需写明FOB金额，运费价格，及C&F总价。		+ SIGNED COMMERCIAL INVOICE IN TRIPLICATE ORIGINAL AND MUST SHOW BREAK DOWN OF THE AMOUNT AS FOLLOWS: FOB VALUE, FREIGHT CHARGES AND TOTAL AMOUNT C AND F.
开出全套清洁、已装船、凭指示海运提单。注明运费预付，并通知申请人。此外，需写明信用证号以及卸货港货船代理人的全名、地址及电话。 按行业习惯，全套提单一般是三正三副。寄给客户的必须是正本，提单有货权凭证的功能。		+ FULL SET CLEAN ON BOARD BILL OF LADING MADE OUT TO THE ORDER, MARKED FREIGHT PREPAID AND NOTIFY APPLICANT, INDICATING L/C NO.,THE FULL NAME, ADDRESS AND TEL NO. OF THE CARRYING VESSEL'S AGENT AT THE PORT OF DISCHARGE.
6份装箱单（一正五副），全部手签。		+ PACKING LIST IN ONE ORIGINAL PLUS 5 COPIES, ALL OF WHICH MUSTBE MANUALLY SIGNED.
检验（卫生）证书出自C.I.Q.（中国出入境检查和检疫局）并表明：货物适宜人类健康。		+ INSPECTION (HEALTH) CERTIFICATE FROM C.I.Q. (ENTRY-EXIT INSPECTION AND QUARANTINE OF THE PEOPLE'S REP. OF CHINA) STATING GOODS ARE FIT FOR HUMAN BEING.
由中国国际贸易促进委员出具的产地证。并标明制造商名称以及该出口产品为完全国产。 China Council for the Promotion of International Trade (CCPIT or C.C.P.I.T.)		+ CERTIFICATE OF ORIGIN DULY CERTIFIED BY C.C.P.I.T. STATING THE NAME OF MANUFACTURERS AND THAT GOODS EXPORTED ARE WHOLLY OF CHINESE ORIGIN.
产品生产日期不得早于出运期半个月，受益人需确认无误。		+ THE PRODUCTION DATE OF THE GOODS NOT TO BE EARLIER THAN HALF MONTH AT TIME OF SHIPMENT. BENEFICIARY MUST CERTIFY THE SAME.
需由集装箱按常规航线运输。装运公司的证明书需同其他文件一同提交。		+SHIPMENT TO BE EFFECTED BY CONTAINER AND BY REGULAR LINE. SHIPMENT COMPANY'S CERTIFICATE TO THIS EFFECT SHOULD ACCOMPANY THE DOCUMENTS.
DD. CONDITIONS 议付时基于本证的每个不符点加征50美元的费用。 该费用将从总额中扣除。	47A	ADDITIONAL CONDITION: A DISCREPANCY FEE OF USD 50.00 WILL BE IMPOSED ON EACH SET OF DOCUMENTS PRESENTED FOR NEGOTIATION UNDER THIS L/C WITH DISCREPANCY. THE FEE WILL BE DEDUCTED FROM THE BILL AMOUNT.
CHARGES 在KSA(沙特)境外发生的所有费用及佣金由受益者负担。包括偿付，银行手续费，不符费（如有）及快递费用。	71B	ALL CHARGES AND COMMISSIONS OUTSIDE KSA ON BENEFICIARIES' ACCOUNT INCLUDING REIMBURSING, BANK COMMISSION, DISCREPANCY FEE (IF ANY) AND COURIER CHARGES.

Continued

CONFIRMAT INSTR (confirmation Instructions) 保兑指示	*49	WITHOUT
REIMBURS. BANK Reimbursement 偿付行	53D	MITSUBISHI UFJ FINANCIAL GROUP, JAPAN TOKYO (HEAD OFFICE)
INS PAYING BANK Instructions to the Paying Bank 对付款行的指示	78	DOCUMENTS TO BE DESPATCHED IN ONE LOT BY COURIER. ALL CORRESPONDENCE TO BE SENT TO ALRAJHI BANKING AND INVESTMENT COPRORATION RIYADH (HEAD OFFICE) 所有单据必须一次性快递给开证行。
SEND REC INFO SENDER 发报行 RECEIVER 收报行	72	REIMBURSEMENT IS SUBJECT TO ICC URR 525 根据 ICC URR 525 解释偿付
TRAILER		ORDER IS <MAC:><PAC:><ENC:><CHK:><TNG:><PDE:> MAC:E55927A4 CHK:7B505952829A

BILL OF EXCHANGE

No. ———****————

For_____USD 1,757,800_____ _____
      (amount in figure)   (place and date of issue)

At_____AT SIGHT_____ sight of this   FIRST   Bill of exchange (SECOND being unpaid) pay to_____TO THE ORDER OF BANK OF CHINA, FUZHOU BRANCH_____or order the sum of

ONE MILLION, SEVEN HUNDRED FIFTY SEVEN THOUSAND AND EIGHT HUNDRED US DOLLARS ONLY_____

                        (amount in words)

Value received for_____USD 1,757,800_____of GANODEMA SINENSE & GANODEMA LUCIDUM
              (quantity)   (name of commodity)

Drawn under_____MITSUBISHI UFJ FINANCIAL GROUP, JAPAN_____

L/C No._____0011LC123756_____ dated_____March 20th 2022_____

To: MITSUBISHI UFJ FINANCIAL GROUP, JAPAN   For and on behalf of

                                          FUJIAN XIANZHILOU NUTRA-INDUSTRY
                                          BLDG9, INNOVATION PARK, FUZHOU,
                                          HIGH-TECH ZONE, SHANGJIE, MINHOU,
                                          FUZHOU, FUJIAN, CHINA 35000

                                                 (Signature)
                                                 LI WEI

Appendix Two

COMMERCIAL INVOICE

From: FUJIAN XIANZHILOU NUTRA-INDUSTRY CO., LTD.
Add.: BLDG9, INNOVATION PARK, FUZHOU, HIGH-TECH ZONE, SHANGJIE, MINHOU, FUZHOU, FUJIAN, CHINA 350000

Invoice No.: XZL22NB001
Invoice Date: Mar. 28th, 2022

To: SOUTH AFRICA SPROUT INTERNATIONAL CORP., JAPAN BRANCH

Term of Payment: L/C Payment
Port of Loading: Fuzhou, China
Port of Destination: Tokyo, Japan

CIF Tokyo, Japan by Sea

Commodity	N.W.	Quantity	U/Price	Amount
Ganoderma Lucidum	13,884kgs	13,884kgs	USD 100.00	USD 1,388,400.00
Ganoderma Sinense	1,847kgs	1,847kgs	USD 200.00	USD 369,400.00
Total:				USD 1,757,800.00

Shipping marks: N/M
L/C No. 0011LC123756

	INVOICE NO.	DATE
	XZL22NB001	Mar. 28th, 2022

ISSUER FUJIAN XIANZHILOU NUTRA-INDUSTRY CO., LTD. BLDG9, INNOVATION PARK, FUZHOU, HIGH-TECH ZONE, SHANGJIE, MINHOU, FUZHOU, FUJIAN, CHINA 350000			**PACKING LIST**			
TO SOUTH AFRICA SPROUT INTERNATIONAL CORP., JAPAN BRANCH			INVOICE NO. XZL22NB001		DATE Mar. 28th, 2022	
Commodity Specification	Container No.	Quantity	Carton	N.W	G.W	Meas.
Ganoderma Lucidum	GESU6738383	13,884kgs	1,157	13,884kgs	18,935kgs	224.1m³
Ganoderma Sinense Shipping marks: N/M L/C No. : 0011LC123756		1,847kgs	124	1,847kgs		
TOTAL:		15,731kgs	1,281 Cartons	15,731kgs	18,935kgs	224.1m³
TOTAL IN WORDS:	ONE THOUSAND TWO HUNDRED EIGHT-ONE CARTONS ONLY					

LOGISTICS
ALEM
SALEM LOGISTICS CO., LTD.

------------------------ ORIGINAL ------------------------

BILL OF LADING

Shipper FUJIAN XIANZHILOU NUTRA-INDUSTRY CO., LTD. ADD. :BLDG 9, INNOVATION PARK, FUZHOU HIGH-TECH		
Consignee TO ORDER		
Notify Party (Complete name and address) SOUTH AFRICA SPROUT INTERNATIONAL CORP., JAPAN BRANCH		
Place of Receipt	Precarriage By FUZHOU, CHINA	Excess Value Declaration: Refer to Clause 6(4)(B)+(C) on reverse side
Vessel & Voy. No JI YUAN V.2207	Port of Loading FUZHOU, CHINA	Inland Routing(for the Merchant's reference only)
Port of Discharge: NAGOYA	Place of Delivery: NAGOYA	Final Destination(for the Merchant's reference only)

Particulars furnished by the Merchant

Container No. And Seal No.	Quantity And	Description of Goods	Measurement (CBM)
N/M F0SU8001795/JZL214661/40'HQ GESU6738383/JZL214663/40'HQ TOTAL NUMBER OF CONTAINERS OR PACKAGES (IN WORDS)	1281 CARTONS	4X40'HQ(FCL) CY-CY S.T.C. Ganoderma Sinense Ganoderma Lucidum SHIPPER'S LOAD., COUNT & SEAL FREIGHT PREPAID SAY FOUR FORTY-FT. HQ CONTAINERS ONLY.	18935KGS, 224.1CBM SHIPPED ON BOARD 19th APRIL 2022 L/C No. : 0011LC123756
FREIGHT & CHARGES	Revenue Tons	Rate	Prepaid	Collect
Service Type	Exchange Rate		Prepaid at	Payable at

RECEIVED by the Carrier the Goods as specified above in apparent good order and condition unless otherwise stated, to be transported to such place as agreed, authorized or permitted herein and subject to all the terms and conditions appearing on the front and reverse of the Bill of Lading to which the Merchant agrees by accepting the Bill of Lading, any local privileges and customs notwithstanding.
The particulars given above as stated by the shipper and the weight, measure, quantity condition contents and value of the Goods are unknown to the carrier.

In WITNESS whereof three original Bills of Lading has been signed of not otherwise stated before one of which to be completed the other(s) to be void. If required by the Carrier three original Bills of Lading must be surrendered duly endorsed in exchange for the Goods or delivery order.

Number of Original B(s)/L THREE(3)	Place of B(s)/t Issue/Date CHINA	*SALEM LOGISTICS CO., LTD.*
B/L No. SMLF2202001	Laden on Board the Vessel	*For and* nn SALFM LOGISTICS 3.. I J.
For delivery of goods please apply to SHINKAWA NMF BUILDING 9F 22-13 SHINKAWA CHUO-KU, TOKYO 104-0033 JAPAN imp-east@oceanlinks.co.jp		By--- AS CARRIER

1. Exporter	FUJIAN XIANZHILOU NUTRA-INDUSTY CO., LTD.BLDG 9, INNOVATION PARK, FUZHOU HIGH-TECH ZONE, SHANGJIE, MINHOU, FUZHOU, FUJIAN, CHINA 35000	Certificate No. C226692523810004 **CERTIFICATE OF ORIGIN OF** **THE PEOPLE'S REPUBLIC OF CHINA**	
2. Consignee	SOUTH AFRICA SPROUT INTERNATIONAL CORP., JAPAN BRANCH		
3. Means of transport and route	ON APR. 19TH, 2022 FROM FUZHOU CHINA TO TOKYO, JAPAN BY SEA	5. For certifying authority use only ISSUED RETROSPECTIVELY	
4. Country / region of destination	JAPAN		
		Verification:origin.customs.gov.cn	
6. Marks and numbers N/M	7. Number and kind of packages;description of goods ONE HUNDRED AND TWENTY FOUR (124) CARTONS GANODERMA SINENSE ONE THOUSAND ONE HUNDRED AND FIFTY SEVEN (1157) CARTONS OF GANODERMA LUCIDUH *** *** *** *** ***	8. H.S.Code 12.11 12.11	9. Quantity 1847KGS 13884KGS N.W.	10. Number and date of invoices XZL22NB001 MAR. 28th, 2022
11. Declaration by the exporter The undersigned hereby declares that the above details and statements are correct, that all the goods were produced in China and that they comply with the Rules of Origin of the People's Republic of China. Fuzhou, China, Apr. 21st,2022 -- Place and date,signature and stamp of authorized signatory	12. Certification It is hereby certified that the declaration by the exporter is correct. Fuzhou, China, Apr. 21st,2022 -- Place and date,signature and stamp of authorized signatory			

华泰财产保险有限公司
Huatai Property & Casualty Insurance Co., Ltd.
全国统一服务热线 CUSTOMER SERVICE HOTLINE: 4006095509

货物运输险保险单
CARGO TRANSPORTATION INSURANCE POLICY

正本(ORIGINAL)
保单正本份数: 1
Number of original

保险单号 Policy No.:
BC32N135012200006437

华泰财产保险有限公司或下列签章分公司(以下简称本公司)根据投保人/被保险人的要求,在投保人/被保险人向本公司缴付约定的保险费后,根据后附条款及其他特约条款按本保险单列明的承保条件承保下述货物运输保险,特立本保险单。
This insurance policy witnesses that Huatai Property & Casualty Insurance Co., Ltd. and its undersigned branch office (hereinafter called "this Company"), at the request of the Applicant/Insured and in consideration of the payment to this Company by the Applicant/Insured of the agreed premium, undertakes to insure the under mentioned goods in transportation subject to the conditions of this policy as per the clauses and other special clauses attached hereon.

被保险人: Insured	SOUTH AFRICA SPROUT INTERNATIONAL CORP., JAPAN BRANCH		
提单号: B/L No.	SMLF2202001	发票号: Invoice No.	XZL22NB001
标记 Marks & Nos	包装及数量 Package & Quantity	保险货物项目 Description of Goods	
N/M	1281 CARTONs	Ganoderma sinense Ganoderma Lucidum	
保险金额: Total Amount Insured	USD 1,933,580		
保费: Premium	As ARRANGED		
运输工具: Per Conveyance	JI YUAN 2207	起运日期 slg. on or abt.	Apr. 19, 2022
运输路线: Route 自 From	FUZHOU, CHINA	经 Via	至 To TOKYO, JAPAN

承保条件 Terms and Conditions
Covering All Risks as per Ocean Marine Cargo Clauses of Huatai Insurance Company of China Limited 【2009】N201.

特约约定 Special Conditions:
1. Deductible: 0.5% of total sum insured any one accident. 2. 对于外包装完好情况下货物的腐烂、变质的损失,本保险不承担赔偿责任。

所保货物,如发生保险单项下可能引起索赔的损失或损坏,应立即通过邮件通知本公司claim@ehuatai.com,或者通知本公司的下述代理人。代理人在案件调查和现场查勘前应通知本公司进行确认。若如下代理人无法联络,请拨打本公司客户服务电话 +86 40060-95509 查询。 In the event of loss or damage to the insured cargo which may result in a claim under this Policy, immediate notice should be given to the Company via Email: claim@ehuatai.com or the Company's agent as mentioned hereunder. The Agent shall notify insurance company prior to claim investigation and onsite inspection. If it couldn't be reached, please call +86 40060 95509 for inquiry.

Cornes & Co Ltd 5th Floor, Meikai Building 32 Aakashi-Machi Chuo ku, Kobe 650-0037 〈br〉TEL:(81) 78 3323421 〈br〉FAx:(81) 78 3323070
Tel:(81) 78 3323421 Fax:(81) 78 3323070

华泰财产保险有限公司
HUATAI PROPERTY AND CASUALTY
INSURANCE COMPANY LIMITED

偿付地点 Claim payable at	TOKYO, JAPAN IN USD				
签单公司:	华泰财产保险有限公司 山东分公司 HUATAI PROPERTY & CASUALTY INSURANCE CO., LTD Huatai Property & Casualty Insurance Co., Ltd. shandong Branch		授权代表签字 Authorized signature		
签单日期: Issuing Date	2022-04-18	地址: Add.	济南市历下区经十路13777号中润世纪城17号楼1201		
业务经办: Handler		电话/传真: Tel & Fax		制单: Operator	贾××
				核保: underwriter	贾××

中华人民共和国出入境检验检疫
ENTRY-EXIT INSPECTION AND QUARANTINE OF THE PEOPLE'S REPUBLIC OF CHINA

健康证书
HEALIH CERTIFICATE

发货人名称及地址 Name and Address of Consignor	FUJIAN XIANZHILOU NUTRA-INDUSTRY CO., LTD. BLDG 9, INNOVATION PARK, FUZHOU HIGH-TECH ZONE, SHANGJIE'MINHOUJFUZHOU, FUJIAN, CHINA 350108		
收货人名称及地址 Name and Address of Consignee	SOUTH AFRICA SPROUT INTERNATIONAL CORP., JAPAN BRANCH		
品名 Description of Goods	GANODERMA LUCIDUM/GANODERMA SINENSE		
加工种类或状态 State or Type of Processing	SOLID STATE	标记及号码 Mark & No.	N/M
报检数量/重量 Quantity/Weight	Declared **13884KGS/ **1847KGS		
包装种类及数量 Number and Type of Packages	**1157CTNS/**124CTNS		
贮藏和运输温度 Temperature during Storage and Transport	NORMAL TEMPERATURE		
加工厂名称、地址及编号(如果适用) Name, Address and approval No.of the approved Establishment (if applicable)	FUJIAN XIANZHILOU BIOLOGICAL SCIENCE AND TECHNOLOGY CO., LTD. 6 CHUANGXIN ROAD, FUZHOU HIGH-TECH ZONE, FUZHOU, FUJIAN, CHINA 350108		
启运地 Place of Despatch	FUZHOU, CHINA	到达国家及地点 Country and Place of Destination	NAGOYA, JAPAN
运输工具 Means of Conveyance	BY SEA	发货日期 Date of Despatch	18th Apr 2022
检验结果 Results of Inspection.:	The above-mentioned goods are in conformity with the sanitary requirements and fit for human consumption.		

印章　　　　签证地点 place of issue FUZHOU　　　　签证日期 date of issue 18th Apr 2022
Official stamp　　授权签字人 authorized officer WU BO　　　签　名 signature

中华人民共和国出入境检验检疫
ENTRY-EXIT INSPECTION AND QUARANTINE OF THE PEOPLE'S REPUBLIC OF CHINA

植物检疫证书
PHYTOSANITARY CERTIFICATE

发货人名称及地址 Name and Address of Consignor	FUJIAN XIANZHILOU NUTRA-INDUSTRY CO., LTD.BLDG 9, INNOVATION PARK, FUZHOU HIGH-TECH ZONE, SHANGJIE'MINHOUJFUZHOU, FUJIAN, CHINA 350108		
收货人名称及地址 Name and Address of Consignee	SOUTH AFRICA SPROUT INTERNATIONAL CORP., JAPAN BRANCH		
品名 Name of Produce	SEE ATTACHMENT	植物学名 Botanical Name of Plants	SEE ATTACHMENT
报检数量 Quantity Declared	SEE ATTACHMENT	标记及号码 Mark & No.	N/M
包装种类及数量 Number and Type of Packages	SEE ATTACHMENT		
产地 Place of Origin	SEE ATTACHMENT		
到达口岸 Port of Destination	TOKYO, JAPAN		
启运地 Place of Despatch	FUZHOU, CHINA		
运输工具 Means of Conveyance	BY SEA	检验日期 Date of Inspection	18th Apr 2022

兹证明上述植物、植物产品或其他检疫物已经按照规定程序进行检查和/或检验，被认为不带有输入国或地区规定的检疫性有害生物，并且基本不带有其他的有害生物，因而符合输入国或地区现行的植物检疫要求。

This is to certify that the plants, plants products or other-regulated articles described above have been inspected and/or tested, according to appropriate procedures and are considered to be free from quarantine pests specified by the importing country/region, and practically free from other injurious pests; and that they are considered to conform with the current phytosanitaiy requirements of the importing country/region.

杀虫和/或灭菌处理 DISINFESTATION AND/OR DISINFECTION TREATMENT

日期 Date	***	药剂及浓度 Chemical and Concatenation	***
处理方法 Treatment	***	持续时间及温度 Duration and Temperature	***

附加声明 ADDITIONAL DECLARATION

****

印章　　　　　签证地点 place of issue <u>FUZHOU</u>　　　　签证日期 date of issue <u>18th Apr 2022</u>
Official stamp　授权签字人 authorized officer <u>WU BO</u>　　　签　　名 signature

ATTACHMENT:

证书
CERTIFICATE

正本
ORIGINAL
共2页第2页 Page 2 of 2
编号No.:222000000562584002

ATTACHMENT

序号 NO.	品名 Name of Produce	植物学名 Botanical Name of Plants	报检数量 Quantity Declared	包装种类及数量 Number and Type of Package	产地 Place of Origin
1	GANODERMA LUCIDUM	***	**13884KGS	**1157CTNS	FUZHOU, CHINA
2	GANODERMA SINENSE	***	**1847.6KGS	**124CTNS	FUZHOU, CHINA

****